# *SPIZZERINCTUM*

*A true story about the baptism in combat and gallantry in action of the Vietnam-era citizen soldiers of the 4th Infantry Division*

By

**DOUGLAS BARR**

**Lieutenant Colonel,**

**U.S. Army (Retired)**

Published by DHB Publishing
Steilacoom, WA 98388

ISBN 9798871053829

**SPIZZERINCTUM**

First Edition, December, 2023

## Review:

*"General Westmoreland shouted "Spizzerinctum!" to our West Point class, meaning have the intestinal fortitude to succeed! Doug Barr tells the story of our class as we went to war not from his point of view but that of his classmate, Al Palmer, providing a unique perspective that pulls the reader forward."*

Tom Anthony – Amazon Best-Selling Author

## Acknowledgments:

I wish to thank Combat Infantry Veteran Bill Comeau for the valuable contributions he has made to this story. His historical writings, periodic band-of-brothers newsletters, and personal stories that recount his Battle of Suoi Tre experiences have made it possible to bring this story to life.

I wish to thank Bob Babcock, Historian of the 4th Infantry Division, for pointing me to historical documents related to the Battle of Suoi Tre and for introducing me to Bill Comeau.

## Dedication:

-- This story is dedicated to the young soldiers of the 4th Infantry Division in Vietnam, - to honor their service, their sacrifice and their gallantry in action. --

# TABLE OF CONTENTS

## PREFACE

This is a true story of young American Soldiers' Baptism in Combat.

It honors the memories of the young American Soldiers who served in the Vietnam War. These are the soldiers who fought the war at the company-grade level – the privates, corporals, and sergeants – the lieutenants and captains. It honors the memories of their extreme sacrifices while they did their duties as citizen-soldiers to fight a tough and determined enemy in a very difficult jungle environment.

It does not honor the righteousness of the Vietnam war, but it does honor the memories of the soldiers who fought it. They deserve to be recognized and memorialized for their bravery and extreme sacrifices. This story provides just one example of the grit, indomitable spirit and outstanding performance of the post-WWII generation of American soldiers during the 1960's in Vietnam.

Much has been said about the dedication and sacrifice of the WWII soldiers, sailors, marines, and airman and women of the "Greatest Generation" - and rightfully so. The WWII "Greatest Generation" set the finest example for all Americans to achieve. Prior to the Vietnam War, General Douglas MacArthur described the American soldiers' history and indomitable spirit when he spoke to the West Point Corps of Cadets on May 12th, 1962:

*"… And what sort of soldiers are those you are to lead…. when I think of his patience under adversity, of his courage under fire, and of his modesty in victory, I am filled with an emotion of admiration I cannot put into words. He belongs to history as furnishing one of the greatest examples of successful patriotism; he belongs to posterity as the instructor of future generations in the principles of liberty and freedom; he belongs to the present, to us, by his virtues and by his achievements…."* [1]

From this WWII generation of brave soldiers emerged yet another generation of American citizen soldiers who were greatly influenced by the legacy of the "Greatest Generation." These young soldiers of the next generation were the sons, daughters, nephews, and youngsters who were born and raised during and immediately after WWII. They had been raised in an environment of American patriotism that followed WWII. This generation of soldiers came of age in the 1960s during the tumultuous period of the Vietnam War.

James Webb Jr., the former Secretary of the Navy, was one of these patriots from this next generation who served bravely and nobly in Vietnam. The following are some of his words describing this next generation of patriots:

*"Few who served during Vietnam ever complained of a generation gap. The men who fought World War II were their heroes and role models. They honored their father's service by emulating it, and largely agreed with their father's wisdom in attempting to stop Communism's reach in Southeast Asia….*

*"Dropped onto the enemy's terrain 12,000 miles away from home, America's citizen-soldiers performed with a tenacity and quality that may never be truly understood."* [2]

This is a true story about some of these young American soldiers, and their baptism in combat in Vietnam. It follows the experiences of two young soldiers assigned to the famous 4th Infantry Division – Infantry Captain Allyn Jon Palmer and his Radio Operator (RTO), Infantryman Bill Comeau, along with their fellow soldiers. It follows these soldiers as they progressed through their Army preparation for combat at Ft. Lewis, Washington, and their subsequent deployment to Vietnam.

It describes their unexpected involvement in one of the largest and most epic battles in Vietnam – the Battle of Suoi Tre on March 21st, 1967.

# Chapter 1 - Prelude to the Battle of Suoi Tre

Deep in the Vietnam Jungle of War Zone C –

Twilight had just begun on March 20, 1967. The sun was just going down deep in the Vietnam jungles of War Zone C. The 3rd Battalion of the 22nd US Infantry Regiment, part of the 3rd Brigade of the 4th Infantry Division (4th ID), had just established a large defensive perimeter named Fire Support Base (FSB) GOLD. The 3rd Brigade of the 4th ID was on the hunt for the elite 272nd Viet Cong (VC) Main Force Regiment, part of the 9th Viet Cong (VC) Division. This VC regiment, comprising some 2500 plus enemy soldiers, was believed to be hiding somewhere in this deep jungle area of War Zone C. US intelligence reports indicated the 272nd VC Regiment was preparing to launch a future large surprise attack on vulnerable US forces somewhere in South Vietnam.

The initial plan of the 3rd Brigade was to establish a secure artillery firebase at FSB GOLD which contained a battalion of artillery from the 2nd Battalion, 77th US Artillery Regiment. This artillery battalion was needed at FSB GOLD to provide a base of supporting artillery fires to the infantry soldiers who would be operating in the surrounding jungle areas to locate and engage the 272nd VC Regiment. The next step was to locate, engage and destroy the VC regiment using US infantry troops from the 3rd Brigade, 4th ID.

At dusk on March 20th, the 3rd Battalion, 22nd Infantry sent out from FSB GOLD some nighttime security forces. This action was a precautionary measure to provide early warning in the event of a surprise night attack of FSB GOLD by enemy forces. The battalion sent out two reinforced infantry squads as ambush patrols. One squad was positioned several hundred meters to the east where it set up an ambush position. The infantry battalion established their night ambush sites on the most likely enemy avenues of approach to FSB GOLD. Their mission was to disrupt and destroy any enemy forces they encountered approaching FSB GOLD at night. In addition, the battalion sent out small teams of infantrymen to establish night Listening Posts (LPs) approximately 100 meters in the jungle to the east of FSB GOLD. Their mission was to remain on silent listening watch for enemy activity and quietly to alert the 3rd Battalion by radio of any pending surprise attack should they hear suspicious activity during the night.

The two ambush patrols departed the FSB GOLD perimeter after dusk and made their way some 400 meters, one to the east and one to the west, where they set up for the night. One patrol of infantrymen found and occupied some makeshift foxholes they found that would provide them some cover and concealment in the jungle. They first put out their Claymore Mines for protection in the direction of their enemy threat. Then the infantrymen hunkered down in their makeshift foxholes. They stayed awake and alert as the total darkness closed in; per their instructions, they sent situation reports (SITREPs) by radio every hour on the hour back to their headquarters. If everything was quiet, their report on the radio was short, i.e., "Negative SITREP."

It was another hot jungle night. The ambush-patrol soldiers could feel the humidity that sapped their energy; they were wet with sweat; the mosquitoes were terrible and plagued them relentlessly. The night remained quiet. The ambush patrols continued to report negative SITREPs for several hours into the night. Then in the early-morning darkness at around 0429 hours (4:29 AM) the American soldiers occupying the ambush position to the east began hearing sounds of individuals moving in the jungle around them. These were VC soldiers. They were so close that the ambush patrol could smell them. The VC soldiers appeared to be moving with stealth through the jungle towards FSB GOLD. The ambush patrol soldiers remained quiet and whispered their report over the radio of this enemy movement to their Company Commander at FSB GOLD. Then the jungle went quiet again.

At daybreak, 0630 hours (6:30 AM), the American infantrymen decided to return to FSB GOLD. They retrieved their Claymore mines and prepared to move back when they spotted some enemy VC soldiers and opened fire on them with small arms weapons and grenades. The VC soldiers returned fire and began to assault their ambush patrol position. A major firefight had begun.

In the quiet early morning of March 21, 1967, as the ambush patrol fired at the VC soldiers, a large number of VC soldiers quickly responded with a heavy volume of fire; then the

VC soldiers attacked and overwhelmed the outnumbered American soldiers of the ambush patrol. The explosions and gunfire alerted the US forces in FSB GOLD that they were under a pending attack by an unknown-sized enemy force. The Battle of Suoi Tre was about to begin.

For the 4th Infantry Division this began what would turn out to be the largest one-day battle at that point in the Vietnam War in terms of the number of enemy VC soldiers killed in a single day. For the 3rd Brigade of the 4th Division, it turned out to be a monumental and decisive battlefield victory for which the 3rd Brigade was later awarded the Presidential Unit Citation by the President of the United States.

On the eve of this battle and located some 3 kilometers northwest of FSB GOLD, the 2nd Battalion of the 12th Infantry Regiment had just settled into its night defensive positions in the deep jungle. The Alpha (A) Company Commander, twenty-four-year-old Captain Jon Palmer, had just received his platoon's night-time situation reports from his Radio Telephone Operator (RTO) and right-hand man, nineteen-year-old Infantryman Bill Comeau.

Just 2 years and 9 months earlier Captain Palmer had graduated from West Point with the Class of 1964. At that time, he was commissioned a Second Lieutenant in the Infantry Branch. Little did he know that in such a short time he would be a Captain, commanding an infantry company of 160 soldiers in jungle combat. Twenty-four-year-old Captain Palmer had received an unexpected early promotion to the rank of Captain because of the high loss of Captains in Vietnam due to battle casualties. He had expected to reach Captain in four years and was surprised to reach this rank so quickly - one year and three months ahead of schedule.

With Captain Palmer on that night in the jungle was his reliable RTO, Infantryman Bill Comeau. Specialist Comeau had been one of the young civilian draftees sent to Ft. Lewis in early 1966 to be quickly trained for combat. He was a factory worker when he was drafted in December of 1965. He had been sent to Fort Lewis where he was assigned to Alpha (A) Company, 2nd Battalion, 12th Infantry Regiment for combat training and subsequent deployment to Vietnam. That is where he met up with then-Lieutenant Jon Palmer.

This story follows these two young infantry soldiers and their fellow soldiers of the 3rd Brigade, 4th Infantry Division as they evolved on their journey from civilians to Vietnam combat soldiers at the epic Battle of Suoi Tre.

# Chapter 2 – West Point Graduation Day

It was the 3rd of June 1964. Graduation day had finally arrived for Allyn Jon Palmer and his West Point "Class of 1964" – this was the proudest day for the 565 graduating members of the West Point Class of '64. Together they had endured four long years of austere military life, education, and training at West Point - their "Rockbound Highland Home." During that time, they had climbed that slippery mountain of West Point and had finally reached the top together. The Class of '64 rejoiced together on that eventful day.

While at West Point, the "Class of 1964" had also formed a close bond with General William "Westy" Westmoreland. This special Class of '64 bond with "Westy" developed when the general began his duty as the new West Point Superintendent at the very same time the Class of '64 began their duty as new cadets. In effect, they both began a new journey at West Point together. It soon became clear that "Westy" felt a special connection with the Class of '64.

Upon his departure from West Point in 1963, "Westy" made some special farewell remarks to the class. In his remarks he included a special word he coined signifying his unique bond with the Class of '64. The word was: "SPIZZERINCTUM." If you ask any member of the West Point Class of '64 about that strange word, he will remember it came from "Westy" to the class as a rallying cry signifying the special connection "Westy" had with the Class of '64. That special connection continued on in the years that followed after West Point. Soon the new graduates of the Class of '64 would find themselves serving again with General Westmoreland in Vietnam.

The all-male West Point Class of '64 was about to begin the next phase of their professional lives – military duty as Second Lieutenants in the Armed Forces of the United States. They all took an oath that day to support and defend the Constitution of the United States against all enemies, foreign and domestic. Their starting salary as a new Second Lieutenant was $222.15 per month, plus a quarters allowance of $85 and ration allowance of $47.88, for a total of $355.03 a month.

Most of the class were commissioned on that day as Second Lieutenants in the U.S. Army. This would lead them eventually to Vietnam. The next step for them, however, would be to undergo physically rigorous Army Airborne and Ranger training at Fort Benning, Georgia, the "Home of the U.S. Infantry." As brand-new Army Second Lieutenants they generally looked forward to this training with optimistic enthusiasm. It was a welcomed change from West Point cadet life, and it would be their first real challenge as new second lieutenants. At Fort Benning they would be learning valuable combat skills before reporting to their first regular army combat units. They looked forward to the challenge.

Upon completion of their Airborne and Ranger training at Fort Benning, each new second lieutenant would report to a regular army tactical unit to begin his first real duty assignment. The duty assignments varied. Some were located in West Germany; others were located in Korea, Okinawa and Panama; many were located at U.S. Army posts spread throughout the United States.

Fort Lewis, Washington, was one of these Army posts designated for duty assignments. At the time it was the home base for the famous 4th Infantry Division. After Airborne and Ranger training, some 44 of these new second lieutenants from the West Point Class of '64 travelled to Fort Lewis, Washington to begin their first duty assignments. They joined the 4th Infantry Division to begin their army assignments. Soon this would lead them to Vietnam. One of these new 4th Infantry Division lieutenants was Second Lieutenant Allyn Jon Palmer from the small town of Elkhorn, Wisconsin.

By this time, it was late in 1964, and the Vietnam War was growing in size. Eventually these new lieutenants would find themselves serving in Vietnam, again under General Westmoreland.

During this same time period on the other side of the world, in July of 1964 the first Viet Cong (Peoples Liberation Force) Division, was formed in South Vietnam; it was the notorious 9th Viet Cong (VC) Division. This Division was formed in Tay Ninh province, northwest of Saigon. The division was originally organized from the 271st and 272nd Viet Cong Regiments and additional supporting units. The 273rd Regiment was added soon after. By December 1964 the Viet Cong 9th Division seized the Catholic village of Binh Gia east of Saigon. During the battle, the division ambushed and destroyed a South Vietnamese Ranger battalion and a South Vietnamese Marine battalion. [1]

In less than three years' time from Jon Palmer's graduation day, this notorious VC unit would initiate an epic battle with the 3rd Brigade of the American 4th Infantry Division, to which Jon Palmer was assigned. It was a real baptism in battle for the young soldiers of the 3rd Brigade, including Captain Jon Palmer, his RTO Bill Comeau, and the men of Alpha Company, 2nd Battalion, 12th Infantry Regiment.

# Chapter 3 - Allyn Jon Palmer's Journey to West Point

Allyn Jon Palmer was born in Elkhorn, Wisconsin, in March of 1942. The county hospital was about 20 miles from the dairy farm where he grew up. The nearest town was Zenda, Wisconsin, named for the classic novel, The Prisoner of Zenda, written by Anthony Hope in 1894. The population of Zenda was about 100 people when Allyn was growing up. His parents wanted to name him Jon Allyn Palmer, but they decided against it when they realized what his initials would spell. It was just too soon after the Japanese attack on Pearl Harbor on December 7th, 1941.

Jon Palmer attended Zenda State Grade School which was situated in a two-story building that housed grades one through four on the first floor and fifth through eighth on the second floor. He had the same teacher for his first four grades and another teacher for last four grades. Each of those teachers taught six or seven subjects for each class. The greatest number of kids in his classes was usually either seven or eight. The enrollment each year was based on how many hired hands were needed by area farmers for a particular year and how many children they had to educate. There were only three other students who spent all eight years together with Jon.

There was a railroad that ran right through the middle of Jon's town. It also ran right through the farm where Jon grew up, splitting the farm in half. As a kid, Jon would play on the boxcars that were sometimes parked for two or three days near a feed company waiting to unload fertilizer and offload feed grain. Jon would have great fun climbing all over the boxcars. This was his playground.

On weekends when the feed company was shut down, he would use the boxcars to reach the roof of the feed mill. Once he reached the roof, he would climb through the unlocked upper window and climb inside the grain access to this giant feed mill where he would play hide and seek with his friends for hours at a time.

Jon attended Big Foot High School which was a consolidated regional high school in Walworth, Wisconsin. It was located about seven miles from the farm. The high school had around 400 students, and his graduation class numbered about 90 students. Jon played football and baseball on his high school team. He was a pitcher on the baseball team, and according to him, he threw a lot of "junk." Jon graduated from high school in the top 10% of his class in 1960.

In early 1960 during his senior year, Jon had signed up to attend North Central College in Naperville, Illinois, located 20 miles from Chicago. He had plans to major in engineering because of the reputation the college had developed in that field.

One night Jon's dad was reading the local newspaper and came upon a notice that their Congressional Representative, Gerald T. Flynn, was giving Civil Service exams in order to select nominees for the service academies. His dad suggested he take the test. So Jon took the test and later was notified that he had been selected as the third alternate to go to West Point. He figured that meant he would definitely be attending North Central College.

Two weeks before Jon graduated from high school, he received another letter notifying him that he had been selected to attend the United States Military Academy at West Point, N.Y. His acceptance letter included words that said: "Congratulations, you are fully qualified and have been accepted for entrance to West Point with the Class of 1964." The letter provided other administrative instructions for entrance, when and where to report, etc. Jon was to report on July 5, 1960, to begin his Plebe Year at West Point.

Suffice it to say, Jon was quite surprised to receive this news that he had been accepted to West Point. He decided to accept the appointment to West Point.

Jon was open-minded about the idea of going into the military. He was willing to give it a try. If he liked it, he would make it a career. If not, he would serve his time and then get out. His service commitment after West Point graduation would be four years.

So on July 2nd, 1960, Jon packed his bags and boarded the train at Walworth, Wisconsin, for Chicago and then on to New York City. From NYC he caught the bus for the 50-mile ride up to West Point, N.Y. As his train left the Walworth Station, it took the same tracks that divided his parents' farm, and so he waved farewell as he passed the farm.

On the same train trip Jon met one of his future West Point classmates, Tom Erdman, who was from Racine, Wisconsin. Jon learned that Tom had been designated the second alternate from the same congressional district. It turned out that the primary West Point candidate had declined the opportunity and the first alternate candidate had failed the stringent physical exam. That opened up the opportunity for Jon and Tom to attend West Point. Jon later considered it blind luck that he got into West Point. [1]

# Chapter 4 - Jon Palmer at West Point

At the time of Jon Palmer's entry to West Point in July of 1960, West Point was an all-male military academy whose purpose was to instruct and train West Point Cadets to become career combat officers who would eventually lead soldiers in combat.

## Plebe Year – Jon's First Year at West Point

Plebe Year began when Jon reported for duty on July 5, 1960, to begin the initial two months of summer training known as "Beast Barracks." Over 800 New Cadets reported that day to begin the Beast Barracks ordeal as the new "Class of 1964." Four years later, 565 graduated in the West Point Class of 1964.

..........

## Jon's Beast Barracks, July - August 1960

Beast Barracks was the initial summer trial period during which he and his classmates were referred to as "New Cadets." Beast Barracks took place during July and August, the two hottest and most humid, miserable months of the year at West Point. It was a miserable time to be outside doing anything involving physical activity.

This term Beast Barracks properly reflects the nature of this trial period. It was the most intense, grueling, miserable period endured as a West Point Cadet. The ostensible purpose of Beast Barracks was to teach the basics of military Cadet Life at West Point in an intense type of Basic Training format. Subjects such as marching, handling a rifle, marching with a rifle, rifle marksmanship, care and cleaning of a rifle, manual of arms with a rifle, bayonet drill with a rifle, and other basic military skills were taught. Included also was intense physical conditioning, and a very strong dose of how to follow orders immediately.

This ostensible purpose was part of a larger objective. One objective was to weed out quickly those New Cadets who were too weak or lacked the motivation to endure the intense physical and mental anguish that was part of Beast Barracks. It included physical and mental hazing from the upperclassmen. In short, Beast Barracks was the first phase to wash out those who did not have what it takes to be a Cadet. It served its purpose. Approximately 15% of those who entered Beast Barracks departed West Point by September.

Jon's West Point Yearbook for 1964 described Beast Barracks as follows:

"Our introduction to cadet life came on 5 July 1960. The first words we heard were, "Drop that bag" and so, we began. They pulled our necks in, popped up our chests, and taught us the rudiments of the military. We marched to the barber shop and left the last vestiges of the civilian world there. For the next sixty days, we drilled, exercised, shined and polished, and slept - in class. For the next sixty nights, we cleaned rifles and rooms, and memorized poop. Then came our first "good deal" - the Plebe Hike. We marched in circles, spirals, and squares but always uphill. Its end marked the end of Beast and the beginning of a new ordeal – "Reorganization Week." [1]

## Reorganization Week

After Beast Barracks, Jon's classmates dropped the title of New Cadet and were officially accepted into the "Corps of Cadets" as Cadet 4th Class men. They were now full-fledged "Plebes," or, according to the upperclassmen, the lowest form of life on earth.

They received their new Company assignments within the Corps of Cadets. There were two Regiments in the Corps of Cadets at the time. Jon was assigned to Company I-2 in the Second Regiment. He moved into his new barracks location, known as North Area. It was located on the North side of the Cadet Mess Mall which was in turn adjacent to the main Cadet Barracks Area known as Central Area.

During "Reorganization Week" most of the upperclassmen were still away from West Point. They were wrapping up their Summer Training assignments and would soon return to start the academic year. Thus, West Point was fairly quiet for a few days. That would soon change.

..........

## The First Half of Jon's Plebe Year, September – December 1960

Jon was assigned a room in the North Area barracks for the first half of the academic year. There he met his two new roommates. The three of them spent the day getting their stuff put away and getting the room ready for inspection. They knew that when the upperclassmen returned, they would be inspecting their plebe room and checking the new plebes out closely. Soon there would be ten times more upperclassmen around to inspect, supervise, and harass them.

Surviving the initial scrutiny of the returning upperclassmen was the next big challenge after Beast Barracks. The

upperclassmen would be fresh from their summer experiences. They would be feisty and eager to meet and harass the new Plebes. This would be their entertainment for the next few days.

The day came when all the upperclassmen arrived and moved into their new rooms. The plebes hunkered down in their room trying to keep a very low profile. They could hear all the activity of the upperclassmen outside, moving in around them.

Soon they heard a single, loud knock (bang) on our door. They knew this meant an upperclassman was coming in. They sprung into the Plebe brace position of attention, with their chins smashed into their necks. The door swung open, and there were the new Yearlings, or sophomores, walking in and looking mean. During the previous May, these guys had just completed their Plebe Year. As Yearlings, they were now one year ahead of the new plebes. That meant they were eager to exercise their new upper-class privileges of harassing and dumping on the lowly new Plebes. Some would call it their payback since they had endured their harassment as Plebes for the previous 11 months.

For the next four months, Jon and his roommates managed to survive their academics and the harassment from the upperclassmen. Then came the second half of the academic year, and time to change rooms and roommates.

## Jon's Plebe Christmas - December 1960

As the Christmas holidays approached, all the upperclassmen departed for their Christmas break to celebrate Christmas and New Years with their family and loved ones at home. The Plebes, including Jon, were not allowed to leave West Point to go home for Christmas. This was another Plebe Year austerity test of their determination to complete Plebe Year.

That Christmas at West Point was a quiet and very lonely time for most of the plebes. Many of the plebes were from the Eastern parts of the US. Their families were able to visit them at West Point and spend at least some nice family time with them over the Christmas holidays. Their family visits made their Plebe Christmas restriction much easier for them to bear.

Other plebes were not as fortunate. If their family or friends were unable to travel the long distance to West Point, the plebes spent the holidays alone. It was not pleasant being separated from family and friends during that Christmas, but it was necessary to survive Plebe Year.

..........

# The Second Half of Jon's Plebe Year, January – May 1961

**Jon Palmer's Plebe Year at West Point, 1960 – 1961**

**Shown with his Classmates in Company I-2**

**Jon is the first Cadet in the Fourth Row from the left.**

## The Inauguration of President John F. Kennedy, January 1961

In January 1961, Jon marched with his classmates in President Kennedy's Inauguration Parade on the day John F. Kennedy was inaugurated as our 44th President.

In November of 1960, President John F. Kennedy won the US Presidential Election over Richard Nixon. His Presidential Inauguration took place on January 20, 1961, in Washington D.C. It has been a United States tradition since before the Civil War to have the Cadets and Midshipmen from the Service Academies march past the President in his Presidential Inauguration Parade.

Late in the evening before the Inauguration Day, Jon, as a member of The Corps of Cadets, boarded a special train for a night trip down to Washington D.C. The cadets were to march in his Inauguration Parade the next day. They all caught some sleep on the trip down and arrived very early in the morning of Inauguration Day. They had a bit more time to sleep on the train before their assembly time for the parade formation.

The Corps of Cadets assembled early for the parade with their marching rifles and bayonets. They stood around in the assembly area for the longest time. It was a bitter cold and clear day in Washington, D.C. The cadets were cold and uncomfortable in spite of their wool overcoats and gloves. The Corps of Cadets were positioned first in the order of march of all the service academies to march past The President.

Of the four Service Academies that march in the Presidential Inauguration Parade, the Cadets of the US Military Academy at West Point are always the first in order of precedence. The West Point Cadets are always followed in order by The US Naval Academy Midshipmen, The Coast Guard Academy Cadets, and The Air Force Academy Cadets.

This order of precedence was established based on when the four service academies were established. The US Military Academy was established in 1802, by President Thomas Jefferson. West Point was the first service academy to be established in the US, and hence, the first in order of precedence. It is the oldest US Service Academy to be established in America. It is also the first and oldest Engineering School to be established in the US.

The parade finally started. The Corps of Cadets warmed up once they were able to start marching. They marched past President and Mrs. Kennedy right on schedule and saluted him as they passed.

This was the Inauguration where President Kennedy made his famous pronouncement to all Americans, "Ask not what your Country can do for you - Ask what you can do for your Country."

Those famous words President Kennedy spoke on that cold day in January 1961 resonated with the cadets. They were at the right time and place at the start of their military service to follow his advice. Now Jon was even more inspired to finish his West Point education and to serve his Country as a soldier.

After hearing President Kennedy's challenge to all Americans with those words, Jon thought it was his duty to serve. It would be his way to pay back America for all the freedoms we enjoy. These American freedoms were secured and protected thanks to the sacrifices of The Greatest Generation of Americans who fought and risked it all for America in WWII. Jon wanted to be like those of the Greatest Generation in WWII. He was young and had a lot to learn.

Most people did not realize at this time that by his future actions, President Kennedy would essentially launch "The Vietnam Era" in America. No one could know at the time where that era would take America. No one could foresee the internal conflict and division it would bring to Americans of Jon's generation.

## The Graduation Parade and Jon's Plebe Recognition, June 1961

After 11 long months as a Plebe, the day finally arrived for the 1st Classmen's (Firsties) Graduation Parade, followed immediately by the formal "Plebe Recognition Ceremony."

The day was like a festival for everyone at West Point. The "Firsties" were finally graduating, and each of the other classes was moving up to the next upper-class level. No doubt, the happiest ones were the "Firsties" who were graduating and about to begin their new military careers. Also very happy were the Plebes who were about to be "Recognized" as upper-classmen and accepted into their ranks. It was a very happy day for all.

After the parade, the cadets all marched off The Plain (the parade field) and into the barracks area for the private, formal "Plebe Recognition Ceremony." The Plebes from Jon's Company I-2 were all lined up in a long line, standing at attention. Then, starting with the I-2 1st Classmen followed by the 2nd and 3rd Class-Men, each upperclassman would go down the Plebe line, shake the plebe's hand, and using his first name, say congratulations.

It was one of the proudest and most memorable times at that point in a cadet's life. Jon had done it! He had accomplished his first goal to get through Plebe Year at West Point, and he was now "Recognized." This was a big step closer to his goal to graduate from West Point.

· · · · · · · · · ·

## Yearling Year – Jon's Second Year at West Point

Jon's Yearling Year officially began after the Graduation Parade and Plebe Recognition ceremony. His first action as a Cadet 3rd Classman (Sophomore) was to go on a wonderful 30-day leave, his first summer vacation away from West Point. He could hardly wait to go home again. It was great to be back home again.

After his 30-day summer leave at home, Jon returned to West Point to complete his 60 days of Yearling Summer Training at Camp Buckner, near West Point.

## Yearling Summer Training at Camp Buckner, July - August 1961

Camp Buckner is a private Army Training Area located not far from West Point. The Camp Buckner Base Camp is situated on and around Lake Popolopin. This is a beautiful, secluded lake with a boat dock, swimming beaches, small sail boats for recreation, etc. It has the appearance of a private recreation area.

Numerous small cabins, or bunk houses, are situated around the Base Camp to house the Yearling Cadets during Summer Training. Other buildings included a dining hall, shower and bathrooms, and an activity center where weekend dances, parties, etc., were held.

Although The Camp Buckner Base Camp appears to be a recreation area, the surrounding forests, hills and valleys serve as a rigorous summer training area for the Yearling Cadets.

The Yearling Summer training for the Class of '64 consisted of more advanced military training than the basic military training of Beast Barracks. It also included intense physical training each day, but without the harassment endured during plebe year. Each day for Jon would begin with a military run, in formation, at 6 AM wearing T-shirts, shorts, and combat boots. The run would be concluded with some strenuous log-lifting exercises and The Army Daily Dozen exercises led by Army Drill Sergeants. All this would take place before breakfast.

After breakfast, Jon's class would begin the day's regular training per the Daily Training Schedule. Each day was jam-packed with military training which included outdoor classes followed by practical applications. It was intensely physical, with activities such as day and night land navigation with map and compass, hand-to-hand combat, day and night patrolling, weapons training, running obstacle courses, etc. Frequently, the training extended into and throughout the night.

The weekends were for rest and relaxation. That was when Jon's classmates were able to enjoy the lake and all its facilities. Girls were invited up, frequent dances were held, and good times were had by all.

Jon's West Point Yearbook for 1964 had this to say about Yearling Summer Training at Camp Buckner:

\"After thirty wonderful days of leave we returned to Camp Buckner to learn the art of soldiering. The days ahead were filled with reveille runs, physical conditioning, and lots and lots of dirt and sweat. Each branch had its turn with Infantry taking its turn several times. But that was the week and the weekends were filled with swimming, sailing, golf, and girls.

"Infantry got its last chance with Recondo. Designed to show our limitations, it did just that. It was a week of sawdust pits to fight in, cliffs to climb on, and endless hills to run up. Somehow, we survived it all to return to Camp Illumination - a fitting end to a fine summer." [2]

At the conclusion of the Camp Buckner Summer Training, Jon and his classmates were fresh and invigorated new Yearlings, anxious to meet the new Plebes and to begin their second academic year.

· · · · · · · · · ·

## The First Half of Jon's Yearling Year, September - December 1961

Having just returned from their summer training to begin the academic year, the upper-class cadets were generally in a refreshed and feisty mood as a result of their summer experiences. As new Yearlings, Jon and his classmates had new responsibilities to test the new plebes' performance by grilling them on the plebe information they were required to know, i.e., their "plebe poop." This was part of the plebe weeding out process.

They were also responsible to observe and correct the new plebes whenever they made plebe mistakes, which was very often at first. From their first day at West Point, Plebes were taught five acceptable answers they could give to upper classmen. These answers were: "Yes Sir," "No Sir," "No excuse Sir," "Sir, I do not know," and "Sir, I do not understand." Any extraneous or "puny excuses" given by Plebes beyond that were not acceptable and would bring the wrath of the upper classmen upon them. This was part of the 4th Class System at West Point.

For example, if a Plebe had spent two hours on Friday night spit-shining his shoes for the Saturday Morning Inspection in ranks, and if by accident his classmate stepped on his shoes on the way to inspection and ruined the spit shine, his answer to the inspecting upperclassman who asks, "Why are your shoes not properly shined?" must be, "No excuse, Sir." If the Plebe says, "Sir, my classmate stepped on them," he would be chewed out for giving a "puny excuse." That was part of the Plebe System. Plebes learned to accept their plebe responsibilities and not to make "puny excuses." It was harsh but effective to weed out those who made too many excuses for their actions.

## Jon's Yearling Christmas Break, December 1961

Jon returned back home to Wisconsin on his first Christmas vacation away from West Point. It was a nice relaxing time back home. He took the opportunity to visit with his family and friends again. It was a good time for him.

..........

## The Second Half of Jon's Yearling Year, January - May 1962

## General Douglas MacArthur at West Point

By Yearling Year, Jon's West Point training and experiences had influenced him toward the idea of serving his country in the "profession of arms." He realized that military service as a soldier was a noble and patriotic way to repay his country for the blessings and good fortune of being able to live with freedom in America.

The rich history of West Point since its inception in 1802 and the great service to our country displayed by its famous graduates inspired him and his fellow classmates. One very inspirational moment occurred in the spring of 1962, when five-star General of the Army Douglas MacArthur visited West Point to accept the West Point Thayer Award for distinguished service to the nation.

It was May 12, 1962, when General MacArthur traveled up to West Point from his residence in the Waldorf-Astoria Hotel in New York City to accept this award in front of the Corps of Cadets. The Class of '64 will never forget that day when he gave his acceptance speech to The West Point Corps of Cadets. Jon was a Yearling sitting in Washington Hall, the Cadet Mess Hall. The cadets had just finished their lunch time meal. After a few opening remarks by the West Point Superintendent, General William Westmoreland, "Westy" presented the Thayer Award to General MacArthur.

What followed was an unbelievable and unexpected historic moment. Luckily, it was recorded by someone who had a tape recorder.

General MacArthur approached the podium. The Corps of Cadets then stood up to pay him their respect. After a slight pause, The Corps of Cadets sat down. General MacArthur began to speak in a quiet voice. His remarks were carried over loudspeakers and were being recorded privately on a tape recorder.

*As recipient of the Fifth Annual Sylvanus Thayer Award, presented each year to a citizen with accomplishments in the national interest, General MacArthur addressed Founder's Day Dinner, 1962.*

General MacArthur's acceptance speech was delivered without any notes, or script. He spoke extemporaneously from his heart. It was truly inspirational. He was speaking privately and directly to all of the Cadets, as their great mentor. There were no media there to cover his speech or to record his words that day.

Because he was speaking without notes, there would have been no record of his inspirational speech had it not been for someone who had the foresight to turn on a tape recorder and record his words. There was no expectation that a historic speech was about to be made. It was strictly for and about the West Point Corps of Cadets, from one of the most famous graduates and one of the greatest American military leaders ever.

In his speech, General MacArthur bid his final farewell to The West Point Corps of Cadets with his concluding remarks which follow:

".... The shadows are lengthening for me. The twilight is here. My days of old have vanished tone and tint; they have gone glimmering through the dreams of things that were. Their memory is one of wondrous beauty, watered by tears, and coaxed and caressed by the smiles of yesterday. I listen vainly for the witching melody of faint bugles blowing reveille, of far drums beating the long roll. In my dreams I hear again the crash of guns, the rattle of musketry, the strange, mournful mutter of the battlefield.

"But in the evening of my memory, always I come back to West Point. Always there echoes and re-echoes - Duty - Honor - Country.

"Today marks my final roll call with you, but I want you to know that when I cross the river my last conscious thoughts will be of The Corps, and The Corps, and The Corps.

"I bid you farewell." [3]

*- General of the Army Douglas MacArthur*

Artist Paul Stencke Depicts General MacArthur's Duty - Honor - Country Speech to The Corps of Cadets on May 12, 1962

· · · · · · · · · ·

# Cow (Junior) Year – Jon's Third Year at West Point

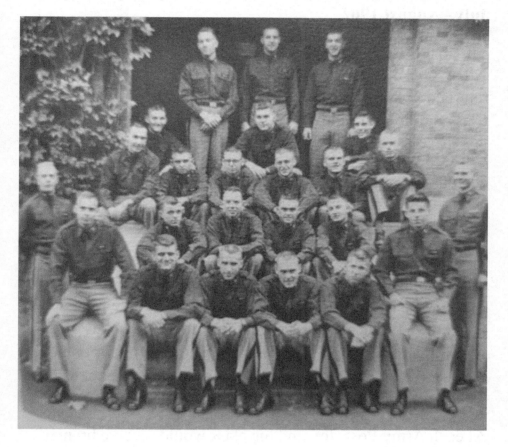

**Jon Palmer's Junior Year at West Point, 1962 – 1963**

**Shown with his Classmates in Company F-2**

**Jon is the fourth Cadet in the First Row from the left.**

## Cow (Cadet 2nd Class) Summer Training, July - August 1962

After Jon's 30-day summer leave back home in Wisconsin, he returned to West Point to complete his 60 days of Cadet 2nd Class Summer Training.

During the first half of this "Cow" summer training, he and his class received from the West Point Military Tactics Department two weeks of military leadership training in and around West Point.

Following that training, his entire class took a class orientation trip, flying to many of the Army Posts around the country. These were Branch Orientation trips which enabled Jon's Class of '64 to learn more about the various Branches of the Army. Each army post they visited was the home for one of the Army branches which the cadets might later select as their career branch after graduation.

At each Army Post, Jon and his class would receive branch orientations and demonstrations which highlighted the branch's purpose, mission, and capabilities. The branch orientations were impressive, and his class was given VIP treatment at each post they visited. The reason was simple: each branch Army Post they visited was trying to persuade and convince them to select their branch as their army career branch.

Jon and his class traveled to the home of the Infantry, Fort Benning, Georgia, for Infantry Branch orientation; to the home of tank warfare, Fort Knox, Kentucky, for Armor Branch and Armored Cavalry orientation; to the home of the Field Artillery, Fort Sill, Oklahoma, for Field Artillery Branch orientation; to the home of the Air Defense Artillery, Fort Bliss, Texas, for Air Defense Artillery Branch orientation; to the home of the Army Engineer Corps, Fort Belvoir, Virginia, for Engineer Branch orientation; and to the home of the Signal Corps, Fort Monmouth, New Jersey, for the Signal Corps Branch orientation.

As a young Cadet, Jon was most impressed by the Infantry Branch at Fort Benning. This was the branch most associated with his notion of the WWII soldier.

At Fort Benning, Jon and his classmates were shown live and dramatic "fire and maneuver" demonstrations of Infantry soldiers and units in action. They experienced the tremendous fire power of the infantry units as they maneuvered in simulated "attack mode" across the Fort Benning countryside.

Later, when it became time for Jon as First Classmen to select his career branch assignment preferences, he chose and received The Infantry Branch as his Army career branch of service.

..........

## Jon's Cow (Junior) Year September 1962 - May 1963

After Yearling Year, all the Cadets in Jon's class switched to different companies, with new company-mates. In this way, they would be able to get acquainted with more of their classmates and make many new friends. It was a good idea, although Jon missed being with his I-2 classmates.

Jon was assigned to Company F-2, still within the 2nd Regiment. In Company F-2 Jon got to know a whole new bunch of his classmates, as well as many other cadets from the other classes.

## Astronaut Frank Borman Lectures on Space Flight

During Jon's Cow Year, the Department of Mechanical Engineering invited Astronaut Frank Borman to provide his Class a lecture and demonstration on his experiences as an Astronaut. This was a part of the Engineering curriculum.

Frank Borman is a graduate of the West Point Class of 1950. At the time he gave his lecture, Frank Borman was an Air Force Major, a Pilot, and an Astronaut-in-training. Later, as the Apollo 8 Commander, he became one of the few Astronauts who flew a mission around the Moon in the late 1960s.

Major Borman made his stage entrance wearing his full astronaut suit. He looked like a robot, and he definitely got the class's attention. Then he took it off and wore his normal pilot flight suit for the duration of his talk and demonstration.

He had on display many of the Astronaut equipment, tools, and gadgets that were to be used in space flight and exploration. He proceeded to explain and demonstrate to Jon's classmates all of these tools and gadgets.

The highlight of his talk was when he pulled out a gadget that looked like a sealed cylindrical drinking container with a large, heavy-duty built-in straw. It was filled with a liquid. He explained that Astronauts drank from this container in space in order to remain hydrated. He then asked for a volunteer from Jon's class to try it out.

**Astronaut Frank Borman**

One of the Army varsity football players volunteered to try it. He was a lineman on the Army Football Team. The cadet took a sip and tasted it in front of the class. "How does it taste?" asked Major Borman.

"Kind of salty," the cadet replied. "What is it?" he asked.

With a straight face, Major Borman replied, "Reconstituted urine."

The Class burst out in laughter. The lineman looked befuddled. Major Borman smiled. It was a good joke.

**Frank Borman – View from the Moon**

..........

## Jon's First Class (Senior) Year –
## His Fourth Year at West Point

In early June of 1963 the West Point Class of 1963 graduated, departed West Point and entered their military service as commissioned officers. At that point Jon and the Class of 1964, officially became Cadet First Classmen. Now his First-Class Year had finally begun.

During Jon's First-Class Year at West Point (1963 -1964), and during the remainder of 1964, the following unrelated history-making events occurred in America:

In November 22$^{nd}$, 1963, President Kennedy was assassinated.

In February of 1964, The Beatles invaded America - they appeared on the Ed Sullivan Show in NYC.

On February 25th, 1964, Cassius Clay upset Sonny Liston and became boxing's Heavyweight Champion of the World.

In November 1964, Lyndon Johnson defeated Barry Goldwater for President of the United States and Commander-in-Chief.

In 1964 President Johnson signed into law the Civil Rights Act of 1964.

In 1964 the World's Fair was held in NYC.

In 1964 Dr. Martin Luther King received the Nobel Peace Prize.

In 1964 the most powerful earthquake in US history at a magnitude 9.2 struck South Central Alaska.

In 1964 President Lyndon Johnson escalated the US Army's involvement in Vietnam.

**Jon Palmer's Senior Year at West Point, 1963 – 1964**

**Shown with his Classmates in Company F-2**

**Jon is the first Cadet in the Second Row from the left.**

## President Kennedy Assassinated During Jon's Senior Year

The morning of November 22nd was a normal day of classes at West Point. The cadets had just finished their last morning classes and were all headed to the noon lunch formation to march to the Cadet Mess Hall for the noon meal. As Jon was leaving his morning class headed to his Cadet Company F-2 area, rumors began circulating that the President had been shot. There was an air of confusion as these rumors circulated and grew among all the cadets. By the time the cadets began their noon meal, it was pretty much confirmed that the President had been shot. There was an air of shock and disbelief among The Corps of Cadets that such a horrible thing could be happening.

Soon thereafter the news was reporting that President Kennedy had died from his wounds. At this point the entire West Point community was in complete shock and disbelief. Just three years prior, Jon and The Corps of Cadets had marched past President and Mrs. Kennedy at his inauguration ceremony in Washington D.C. Just five months prior, President Kennedy had visited West Point and addressed the Class of 1963 with an inspirational speech at their graduation ceremonies. Jon and the Class of '64 were there to witness President Kennedy's visit to West Point. Now President Kennedy was dead. What would happen next?

The annual Army-Navy football game had been scheduled to be played within a few days. President Kennedy had enjoyed attending this classic football rivalry as the President and Commander-in-Chief. The game was quickly postponed in view of his tragic assassination.

President Kennedy had been the youngest man elected President. He was hardly past his first thousand days in office and was the youngest President of the United States when he died.

## The Special Connection to General MacArthur

Jon and his classmates were fortunate as Cadets to hear General MacArthur's inspirational speech delivered privately to The Corps of Cadets in The Cadet Mess Hall at West Point in 1962. They would never forget that speech and the impact it had on the Cadets of West Point then, and even now.

General MacArthur had a very strong connection to West Point and The Corps of Cadets. When he finally retired for good, he lived in The MacArthur Suite of the Waldorf Astoria Hotel in New York City, just 50 miles down the Hudson River from West Point. Apparently, General MacArthur wanted to remain close to West Point.

On his 84th birthday, January 26, 1964, during Jon's senior year, General MacArthur stated that "High honors have come my way, but I shall always believe that my greatest honor was being a West Point graduate."

On that day of his 84th birthday, a contingent of Jon's classmates visited him at his New York City residence to celebrate his birthday. Fortunately, they recorded his remarks on that day. A copy of those remarks were later enclosed in a letter dated 3 February, 1964, from The Commandant of Cadets, General Davison to The Corps of Cadets.

Two months later, on April 5, 1964, General of the Army Douglas MacArthur passed away.

MACC

3 February 1964

MEMORANDUM FOR: Each Cadet, United States Corps of Cadets
Each Officer, Department of Tactics

SUBJECT: Remarks of General of the Army Douglas MacArthur

1. On Sunday, 26 January 1964, it was my privilege to accompany the Superintendent, the Brigade Commander and four other First Classmen to visit General of the Army Douglas MacArthur on his 84th birthday.

2. Following the presentation of formal birthday greetings from the Corps of Cadets by the Brigade Commander, General MacArthur gave extemporaneously a particularly noteworthy message to the Corps. Fortunately, it was recorded. A transcription follows:

"What can I say that has not already been said by me so many times before? High honors have come my way, but I shall always believe that my greatest honor was being a West Point graduate.

The Military Academy taught me many things, some of them not within the covers of books or written by any man. The first of these is Tolerance; not to debase nor deprive those from whom one may differ by character or custom, by race or color or distinction.

The second is Balance; a sense of proportion and ability to put first things first. A realization that there is a time and place for everything, but a recognition of the old maxim, "nothing too much" – what the ancients meant by the "golden mean."

The third is Intelligence, rather than sentiment or emotion. Sentimentalism has muddled many problems, has settled none. Intellect is man's only hope for improvement over his present state.

And last, but by no means least, is Courage; moral courage – the courage of one's convictions – the courage to see a thing through. This is not easy. The world is in constant conspiracy against the brave. It is the age old struggle, of the roar of the crowd on one side and the voice of your conscience on the other.

Tolerance, Balance, Intelligence, Courage. These should be the hallmarks of every graduate of the Military Academy at West Point.

Your visit today has moved me deeply, and to you and to every other member of the Corps of Cadets go my warmest and most affectionate greetings."

3. I know that each of us will be strengthened by these words and encouraged in our endeavor to live by the standards so eloquently expressed by General MacArthur.

MICHAEL S. DAVISON
Brigadier General, USA
Commandant of Cadets

58

## Finally, Graduation

It was the third of June 1964, and the West Point Graduation Week had finally arrived for Jon Palmer. After four long and arduous years of climbing up the slippery mountain of West Point, Jon and his Class of 1964 had finally arrived at the top, and they rejoiced together! Their sense of pride and joy defied description.

**Graduation – The Proudest Moment at West Point**

**Allyn Jon Palmer's Senior Year at West Point, 1963 - 1964**

# Chapter 5 - Jon's Airborne and Ranger Training at Fort Benning

*"People sleep peaceably in their beds at night only because rough men stand ready to do violence on their behalf."*

*George Orwell*

## Jon's 60 Day Graduation Leave

Jon Palmer and his most of his classmates who graduated from West Point were commissioned as Second Lieutenants in the US Army on June 3, 1964. The starting salary as a new Second Lieutenant was $355.18 a month.

Upon graduation, all newly commissioned officers from the Class of '64 were given a 60-day vacation (graduation leave) before they were obligated to report for duty to their first assignment. After four grueling years at West Point, this was unprecedented free time for the new lieutenants to do whatever they pleased for 60 wonderful days. It was a brief time of no stress, no worry.

Many of them attended classmate weddings for those classmates who could not wait to get married. Those weddings were memorable times.

Soon after graduation Allyn Jon Palmer was married to his sweetheart, Sandy, on November 14th in his hometown of Elkhorn, Wisconsin.

## Airborne Training – Jon's First Regular Army Experience

Jon Palmer and the other new Army lieutenants from the Class of '64 attended Army Airborne and Ranger training together at Fort Benning, Georgia.

The first week of Airborne training was called Ground week. Its purpose was:

(1) to get the trainee into top physical condition via daily strenuous exercises and exhausting distance runs in combat boots.

(2) to familiarize the trainee with the soldier harness and parachute equipment worn and operated by the jumper; and

(3) to condition the trainee mentally to react quickly and automatically to do the right things should any parachuting mishaps or emergencies occur during a jump, e.g., main parachute does not open properly, mid-air collisions with fellow parachutists, etc.

The Drill Sergeants who trained the new lieutenants were sadistic bastards who seemed to enjoy making the airborne trainees suffer physically and mentally. This training was so intense physically and mentally that the pain of enduring the training greatly overshadowed the fear of jumping. That was part of the purpose of Ground Week.

Each evening when the day's training was finished, Jon and the other airborne trainees were so exhausted and physically sore that they would crash quickly into their bunks. They needed to get the precious sleep that would help them get through the next day's training.

The second week was called Tower Week. Its purpose was to prepare the trainees physically and mentally for jumping by rehearsing their jumps from first a 34-foot tower, and then from a 250-foot tower.

(Note: Some pictures of Army training shown herein are more recent than 1964)

**Jumping from the 34 Foot Tower**

At the 250-Foot tower, jump trainees would be secured into a harness attached via suspension lines to an open parachute that was connected by a quick release device to a tower hoist. The hoist would then raise the open parachute, with trainee dangling in a harness beneath it, up 250 feet in the air.

With the trainee dangling 250 feet up, the Drill Sergeants on the ground would proceed to harass and mess with him via their megaphone comments yelled up to him. When ready, the Tower Sergeant would then release the parachute with trainee attached so he would experience the 250-foot descent by parachute and then execute his proper "parachute landing fall."

**Jumping from the 250 Foot Tower**

The trainees were told the parachutist impact to the ground was like the impact of jumping off the roof of a car onto the ground. If the parachute landing was not done properly, one could get hurt by the ground impact.

The third week was called Jump Week. Its sole purpose was to make five successful daytime parachute jumps from 1150 feet above the ground out of a military aircraft. This was the culmination of the training so most of the harassment ended during Jump Week.

Now it was all about making five normal and successful jumps. Airborne School Graduation would follow upon successful completion of those five jumps.

The aircraft Jon and his classmates jumped from was a C-119 Flying Boxcar, a Korean War vintage plane. The aircraft fuselage was a compact cabin with two rear doors at angles to the centerline. It had two engines and tail booms which held dual rear stabilizers.

The jumpmaster during each of the five one-way flights was a senior sergeant and experienced paratrooper. During each flight, he had to shout and use hand signals to get the jump commands out to the trainees: "Get Ready" - "Stand Up" - "Hook Up" - "Check Equipment" - "Sound Off for Equipment Check" - "Stand in The Door."

When the aircraft's green "exit" light replaced the red light and the "Go" command was given, Jon proceeded in the line of jumpers ahead of him to the aircraft door. When it was his turn to stand in the aircraft door, he quickly assumed his aircraft exit position and jumped out of the aircraft into the windstream.

The wind force from the aircraft's propellers, or "prop blast," threw Jon backwards toward the tail of the aircraft. The force of gravity pulled him downwards. After two or three-seconds Jon felt a tug on his harness from the aircraft's static line that had pulled open his parachute canopy. The noise and darkness inside the aircraft suddenly changed to bright light and silence, except for the fading engine sounds.

On each jump, Jon would count in his mind for four seconds, (i.e., "one-thousand one, one-thousand two, one-thousand three, etc.) then look up to see if he had any parachute malfunctions. One typical malfunction could be a "Mae West," which makes the parachute canopy look like a large brassiere. An even worse malfunction could be a "streamer" wherein the parachute canopy wraps around itself. In that case, you fall like a rock. Each paratrooper trainee had a reserve parachute attached at the chest just in case of a main parachute malfunction.

On each jump Jon's parachute deployed properly. Now all he had to do was execute a proper parachute landing fall without breaking anything. He looked down at the ground slowly approaching at about 22 feet per second. From that height it took 45 to 60 seconds to reach the ground.

During the parachute's descent on each jump, Jon would look up and around him to avoid collisions with other parachutist who went out the door behind him. On one jump, Jon saw another parachutist above and to the side of him who was descending at a faster rate than Jon. This parachutist was heading directly towards him on a collision course. Jon started yelling loudly for him to "slip away" from him, as he had been trained.

In these situations, trainees were taught to slip the parachute in different directions as the only way to avoid mid-air collisions. The parachutes had four risers which connected to the 30 suspension lines, which in turn connected to the 35-foot-wide nylon canopy. The four risers joined at the jumper's shoulders. By grabbing two risers and pulling down vigorously, a paratrooper could sometimes move laterally in relation to the ground. This action caused the canopy to tilt, spilling air out of the opposite side of the canopy, thereby causing the parachute to drift sideways. To slip right the two right risers were pulled, to slip left the two left risers were pulled.

Each of Jon's five jumps were made during the daytime. It was a standard joke to tell friends who asked later about Airborne Training that all five jumps were night jumps - because he had his eyes closed each time he went out the door.

The highlight of the Airborne Training was the graduation ceremony, during which Allyn and his jump mates were awarded the highly coveted Army Parachutist Badge. Jon wore that badge very proudly for the remainder of his Army career.

**RANGER Training – Jon's Second Regular Army Experience**

After successfully completing his Airborne Training, Jon Palmer attended nine rigorous weeks at The Army Ranger

School. During this Army Ranger Training, Jon was teamed up with a "Ranger Buddy." Each Ranger Candidate had a Ranger Buddy assigned who is another Ranger Candidate. Ranger Buddies were required to stay together always, like brothers. They watched out for each other throughout all the hazardous training exercises. This designation was mostly for safety purposes.

Ranger School was filled with risk. There were many risky actions and events where things could go terribly wrong and cause serious injury or death. Bad things could happen during the night patrols, mountain operations and rappelling, swamp and jungle operations, waterborne operations, etc. Each Ranger Candidate needed a brother whom he can trust to overwatch and support him during these risky times. The Ranger Buddy was the one who helped to minimize the risk of bad things happening.

Jon's nine-week Ranger School was divided into three phases: The Fort Benning Phase, The Mountain Phase, and The Florida Jungle or Swamp Phase. Each phase lasted three weeks.

The Fort Benning phase took place in The Ranger Training Camp, a remote area of Fort Benning, Georgia. This three-week phase consisted of extremely rigorous physical conditioning to build the trainees up physically for the ordeal.

It also included outdoor classes and training in Ranger subjects like combat and reconnaissance patrolling techniques, survival, hand-to-hand combat, mountain climbing, map reading, land navigation (day and night), etc.

The Mountain Phase took place in the mountainous areas around Dahlonega, Georgia. During this three-week phase, Jon and his Ranger Squad lived and worked outside in the local mountains.

Here the Ranger trainees conducted numerous daytime and nighttime combat and reconnaissance patrols, with little sleep or food in between. Part of the training was to wear down the Ranger trainees with food and sleep deprivation to see if they could hold up under those conditions. Those who did not hold up were washed out. What follows is a story of one such wash out.

On one occasion in the Georgia Mountains, Jon's Ranger Squad was conducting a night-time patrol moving through the mountains. The Ranger trainee who was designated as Patrol Leader was being tested on his performance as Patrol Leader: he was responsible for successfully leading and navigating the patrol during complete darkness from their starting point to their next assembly area, which was approximately 1.6 kilometers to the north. The Patrol Leader was being graded on his performance while accomplishing this leadership task.

There was no moon out that night - it was pitch dark and difficult to navigate through the steep ridges and valleys. The Patrol Leader picked the route so it would follow just below a wooded ridge line that would lead them close to their pre-dawn assembly area.

The patrol moved quietly in single file along the ridge line. The Patrol Leader would stop frequently along the way to conduct map checks with a red flashlight under an Army poncho to make sure the patrol was staying on the selected route.

The Patrol Leader was able to navigate the patrol correctly to their next assembly area. The Ranger patrol closed into their pre-dawn assembly area to get some rest before conducting their training-exercise attack at first light on the nearby designated objective. It was very cold, dark, and quiet at the time. Jon lay down on the ground and wrapped up in his poncho to get some sleep.

It was so dark and quiet that the patrol members were not aware that one of their patrol members was sitting nearby on the ground Indian Style. He was sitting up with his legs crossed and he had his poncho draped around him. To keep warm, this trainee had decided to place a small can of sterno camping fuel between his legs near his crotch, and light it up. He draped his Army poncho around himself and sealed it against the ground to keep the flame's heat and light inside his poncho. His head was sticking outside the hood in his poncho. It was a cold October night in the Georgia mountains, and apparently he wanted to be warm and cozy in the cold mountain night air.

The other patrol members were not aware of what this trainee was doing right next to them. They quickly fell asleep. The night continued to be deathly dark and quiet. A few minutes later, the patrol members were awakened by a loud scream.

They opened their eyes and were blinded in the darkness by bright flames coming from the trainees' pants that were burning near his crotch. Apparently, he had fallen asleep, and the flames started to burn his pants. That certainly woke him.

The Ranger trainee was screaming wildly and beating at the flames on his legs and crotch with his hands. Several of the other trainees helped him put out the flames.

He had compromised the entire patrol mission by breaking light and noise discipline. Worse than that, he suffered some fairly serious burns on his hands, legs, and crotch. He had to be medically evacuated to the nearest hospital for treatment of his burns. He was washed out of Ranger School.

During the Mountain Phase, Jon and his Ranger Squad also practiced mountain climbing and rappelling to hone their Ranger skills. During this phase, they were learning how to rappel down steep Georgia mountain cliffs.

The Ranger instructors decided that the rappelling final exam would be for each pair of Ranger Buddies to rappel together down a very high vertical rock cliff. The catch was that one of the Ranger Buddies must be tied with a rope, piggy-back style, to the back of the other Buddy to simulate a mountain rescue situation.

Jon and his ranger Buddy decided that Jon would do the rappelling and his Ranger Buddy would be tied to Jon's back.

As the Ranger Buddy was being tied securely to Jon's back at the top of the cliff, his Ranger Buddy mentioned to Jon that he had better not screw this up. Jon agreed.

As Jon approached the edge of the cliff to rappel, his Ranger Buddy experienced for the first time what it was like to place his life in Jon's hands. It was a long way down to the bottom, and as they inched down the face of the cliff, it seemed as if the rappelling ride on Jon's back would never end.

The Swamp Phase of Ranger School took place in the Florida swamps not too far from Eglin Air Force Base. During this three-week phase, Jon's Ranger Squad lived and worked outside in the local swamps and jungle. Here the Ranger trainees also conducted daytime and nighttime combat and reconnaissance patrols, with little sleep or food in between. Again, part of the training was to wear them down with food and sleep deprivation to see if they could hold up under those conditions. Those who did not hold up were washed out.

**RANGER School – Swamp Phase**

After nine miserable weeks Jon, his Ranger Buddy and his Ranger Squad successfully completed Ranger Training. Jon graduated from The Army Ranger School and was awarded the highly coveted RANGER Tab. He had earned the motto of an Army RANGER – RLTW – Rangers Lead The Way.

**Jon's Army RANGER Squad (all West Point classmates) with the Alligator, "Old One-Eye". Jon is in the top row, last man on the right. Three of his 12 classmates shown here were later killed in Vietnam.**

After successfully completing the Army Airborne and RANGER Schools, Jon had achieved something very special to him: He was qualified as an Army "Airborne Ranger." That did not mean the new Rangers were bullet-proof, but they surely thought they were at the time. They still had a lot to learn about being in combat.

## Jon's Wedding and Trip to Fort Lewis

Following his Airborne and Ranger training at Fort Benning, Jon was next headed to his first Army tactical unit assignment at Fort Lewis, Washington. Jon described this phase of his life as follows:

"Upon (Ranger School) graduation in November, Joe Arnold and I drove straight through to Chicago. Dropped Joe off around 0400 hours on the 12th of November and headed to the farm. I changed into my hunting clothes and was pheasant hunting moments later. Sandy is still upset that I did not come straight to her house and toss rocks at her bedroom window. "

"We had a rehearsal dinner on the 13th, the night before the wedding. They did not have bachelor parties then. We got married the next evening, 14th."

"We took a few days to pack for the movers and say our goodbyes. We set out for our honeymoon on the road heading to Fort Lewis, Washington by car. My first branch selection was for the Infantry, and I chose Fort Lewis, Washington as my destination. I succeeded in getting both preferences."

"Sandy and I arrived at Fort Lewis in late November 1964, just after Thanksgiving. Along the route we got stranded toward night in a blizzard in Big Timber, Montana. Everything was closed except the bowling alley. I braved the snow, and we enjoyed our first Thanksgiving dinner in our motel room eating bowls of chili because that was all the bowling alley had left."

"Upon my arrival at Fort Lewis, I learned that I was being assigned to B Company, 2nd Battalion, 12th Infantry as the Platoon Leader of the First Platoon." [1]

# Chapter 6 - Getting the 4th Infantry Division Ready for Vietnam

## Jon Palmer's First Army Unit Assignment - the 4th Infantry Division (4th ID)

When Jon graduated from West Point, he and about 43 of his classmates were assigned to the 4th Infantry Division (4th ID), at Ft. Lewis, Washington, as their first Army unit assignment. This group of West Point second lieutenants made up a significant number of the company-grade officers in the 4th ID. Since the 4th ID was understrength at the time, a number of these lieutenants were soon given assignments as company commanders. This did not sit well with a significant number of captains who were subsequently assigned to the division. Some of these captains had been to Vietnam, while others had not. Those who lacked company-command time wanted it. They made their feelings known just as the 4th ID was preparing to deploy to Vietnam. The Division Commander, Major General Arthur S. Collins Jr., would have none of that stating, "These lieutenants trained these young recruits, and they will lead them in Vietnam." General Collins personally knew most of these young West Point lieutenants. It made no sense to him to replace these now-experienced company commanders, who knew their units inside-out, with these impatient captains. [1]

When Jon and his new wife, Sandy, arrived at Fort Lewis, Jon was assigned to Bravo Company, 2nd Battalion, 12th Infantry as Platoon Leader of Bravo Company's First Platoon. As a

Second Lieutenant, he served as platoon leader for the first 5 months of his time in the battalion.

One Saturday night the Battalion had a game night which was attended by all the Battalion officers and their wives. They had a potluck dinner followed by playing several different games. Jon won the Scrabble tournament that night. His Battalion Commander took note of that victory. On the next workday, Jon received an order to report to the Battalion Commander. The Battalion Commander told Jon he had noticed his skill at Scrabble and was selecting Jon to be his Battalion Adjutant, i.e., the Battalion Personnel Officer. Jon served in this position until the first week of December 1965, when the Battalion Commander selected him to command his Alpha (A) Company, 2nd Battalion, 12th Infantry. [1] This assignment for Jon was fairly unusual because it was normal for a Captain to command a company. Jon had only just been promoted to First Lieutenant. His selection as company commander reflected the Battalion Commander's confidence in Jon's leadership abilities, even as a brand-new First Lieutenant.

At this time (December 1965) Jon's new company, Alpha Company, was woefully understrength in soldiers. Against an authorized strength of six officers and 160 enlisted men, Alpha Company had only one officer and about 41 enlisted men. All of the 4th ID units were in the same situation, woefully understrength. It turned out that the entire division was about to receive a large influx of new draftees fresh from their initial induction into the Army. These draftees had no Army training whatsoever. This influx of new, untrained soldiers was meant to bring the 4th ID up to full strength rapidly so it could be deployed to Vietnam in the coming months. The problem was that these new 4th ID soldiers were raw recruits, recent draftees who needed to be trained quickly and made ready for combat operations in Vietnam. This was a challenging task. The entire 4th ID had approximately seven months to get these new draftees ready for actual combat. [1]

Lieutenant Jon Palmer's battalion, the 2nd Battalion, 12th Infantry was to receive 800 new draftees to train up quickly before deployment to Vietnam. Jon's Alpha Company would receive 200 of these new soldiers. [1]

During this time, between January through July of 1966, all the 4th ID units were on an accelerated-training timetable. They were quickly brought up to 100% strength with officers and enlisted personnel (i.e., untrained recruits). All units underwent this accelerated training period between January and July of 1966 to get the 4th ID units trained and ready for combat. This training period was unprecedented in the way that it deviated from the normal Army training process for new soldiers.

To bring the 4th ID units up to full strength quickly, the Army bypassed their normal soldier training cycle. The normal process was to provide fresh recruits with Basic Training at an Army Basic Training base, followed later by Advanced Individual Training prior to sending them to their first Army unit. So usually, recruits would get training in the basic Army fundamentals of how to be a soldier, followed by a break in time; then they would be sent to another Army post to receive advanced training in their individual specialty; they would usually get a break in time between each phase of training and prior to reporting to their first Army unit.

The Vietnam accelerated preparation process for the 4th ID sent the untrained recruits immediately after their Army induction directly to Ft. Lewis for their basic and advanced individual training with their first Army unit, the 4th ID in this case. This was an exception to the normal Army training process necessitated by the urgency of being earmarked for deployment to Vietnam. It turned out to be a unique period in the history of the 4th Infantry Division.

Major General Collins had roughly seven months to get the 4th ID units, including Allyn's Alpha Company, trained up and ready for combat - to provide new raw recruits (mostly draftees) with their Basic Training followed by their Advanced Individual Training.

Then the recruits would receive their Basic Unit Training, and Advanced Unit Training. All this training had to be accomplished before the 4th ID would deploy to Vietnam for combat operations. This new process was called "train and retain".

The new recruits of the 2/12th Infantry Battalion arrived knowing little more than how to wear the uniform and follow basic instructions. They had absolutely no Army experience and none of the soldier skills needed for combat in an infantry division.

One of these new recruits assigned to then-Lieutenant Jon Palmer's Alpha Company was Private Bill Comeau from New

Bedford, Mass. Bill Comeau would eventually become Jon Palmer's Radio Telephone Operator (RTO) and trusted right-hand man in Vietnam.

## Bill Comeau's Journey to Fort Lewis and the 4th Infantry Division

By the time Bill Comeau was ready for high school, there was no question that he would get a high school diploma. He knew that he couldn't go to college, but he had the grades which punched his ticket to the local vocational school.

The year was 1960. At thirteen years old, Bill had to choose a profession that he planned to use for the rest of his life. The choices were, Carpentry, Welding, Electrical, Electronics, Steam Engineering, Machine Shop, Automobile Repair, Drafting, Industrial Design, and Household Arts for the girls. Bill chose machine shop since he heard that machinists and especially tool and die makers were in high demand and commanded the highest salaries. What did he know at thirteen?

He graduated from high school with average grades and in 1964 went to work as a Maintenance Technician at a local bakery that produced Sunbeam bread. He left there after a year to work at a factory that produced spare automobile transmission parts. While there, he received his draft notice.

After so many of his extended family had served, Bill thought it was now his time to help defend his country. His mother was very broken-hearted. Her only son was set to be placed in danger in Vietnam.

It was no great surprise when he received his induction notice. He had gone for two physicals at the Boston Army Base previously and he knew it was just a matter of time. He was 19 years old when duty called, and he knew that he would be stepping into the shoes of most of the men of his family who served in World War II or Korea. He believed it was his time to serve.

Things were going pretty well for him in the fall of 1965. He had a car, a good paying job, and a high school sweetheart who had been with him since his sophomore year. Life was about to change radically for him.

At 6 AM on the chilly morning of Monday, December 13, 1965, Bill arrived at the local draft board where the mayor of New Bedford met all the local inductees. There were nineteen draftees there. A representative from the local veterans' organization bid them a fond farewell and hailed them to "Give those commies hell." After receiving their gift of shaving gear from the veterans' representative, the draftees were registered and sent outside to wait for the bus to take them away to the Boston Army base for their initial induction.

As they were waiting for their bus to arrive, the mayor approached Bill's mother who was very upset about what was happening. He told her, "Don't worry, lady. The army is going to take good care of your son."

After initial induction and subsequent Army in-processing at Ft. Dix, New Jersey, Bill and his fellow draftees were given the rank of Private E-1 (with a starting pay of $89.00 per month in 1965). They were then sent off to their next duty stations. It turned out that Bill's next duty station would be Fort Lewis, Washington.

Bill and his fellow inductees boarded busses that evening for a trip to Philadelphia International where they would catch a redeye flight to Seattle-Tacoma Airport. They were on their way to Fort Lewis for basic combat training (BCT), advanced individual training (AIT) and then combat unit training in preparation for deployment to Vietnam. [2]

# Chapter 7 – Training Young Draftees for Vietnam Combat

At Fort Lewis, Major General Arthur Collins, the 4th Infantry Division (4th ID) Commanding General, had been hand-picked to lead the 4th ID's training preparation and deployment to Vietnam on an accelerated schedule. General Collins liked soldier training that was innovative and exciting, especially if it was developed by the unit and for the unit – that is, developed by the squad leaders, platoon sergeants, and platoon leaders. [1]

General Collins also took great interest in the training and welfare of his 4th ID soldiers - and he liked to be around them as much as possible. One of his new 4th ID soldiers later recalled the following story about General Collins:

On a cold, wet day of field training in January 1966, General Collins visited some troops being training to see how the new troops were doing. They were heading to Vietnam soon and he wanted to see if they were learning how to be combat soldiers. The general approached a private by the name of Private Polhan and asked him how things were going.

Private Polhan responded, "Sir, not bad with one exception!" General Collins asked what that exception was. The private's response was, "Well Sir, I'm from Iowa. In farm country, breakfast is a very important meal for us, and I'm not getting enough to eat in the morning here."

General Collins said, "Well Private Polhan, tomorrow morning you tell the mess sergeant that I said you could have another egg for breakfast."

Early the next morning Private Polhan was in the chow line. The Mess Sergeant was frying eggs as the private approached the grill. The private repeated to the Mess Sergeant what General Collins had said to tell him. The Mess Sergeant looked at Private Polhan and after careful consideration placed another egg on his mess kit and said, "Move on, troop." At that moment there was a lot of commotion at the back of the mess tent. Someone announced, "ATTENTION!."

In walked General Collins. The General walked to the chow line where Private Polhan and the Mess Sergeant were still standing. General Collins recognized the private, approached him and said, "I thought I would stop by and see if you got that extra egg this morning."

The Mess Sergeant had beads of sweat on his forehead which could have been from standing over a hot grill, or perhaps from the General's presence.

Private Polhan replied, "YES SIR, THANK YOU SIR!'

The troops were put "AT EASE," and they continued with their morning meal. ₂

One day while then-First Lieutenant Jon Palmer was training his Alpha Company, Four-Star-General Creighton Abrams, the Army Chief of Staff, travelled to Fort Lewis to view some of the 4$^{th}$ ID training activities in preparation for Vietnam. During that day, General Abrams wanted to see some actual training as it was taking place. Major General Collins had selected the Squad Reaction Course that Lieutenant Palmer helped develop for General Abrams to observe. Although everyone was wearing Army combat fatigues, General Abrams arrived at the outdoor training facility wearing his Army Dress uniform with black polished shoes. On this day, the Squad Reaction Course was a mud hole due to recent heavy rains. When General Abrams arrived, he came to Lieutenant Palmer and said, "OK, where is the next squad ready to go?" Lieutenant Palmer said, "There they are, and here they come." General Abrams listened to the squad briefing and when it concluded, the squad moved out with General Abrams, Major General Collins, and Lieutenant Palmer walking right behind them through the mud and gunk. Before too long General Abrams' dress uniform was filthy with mud. The squad performed well and did everything they were trained to do. General Abrams did not seem to mind the muddy mess on his dress uniform. He was a famous WWII cigar-chomping tank soldier who had been in ferocious combat with General Patton in Europe. Obviously, a bunch of mud during combat training was not going to bother him at all. [1]

As Lieutenant Jon Palmer trained these Alpha Company recruits for future combat in Vietnam, he witnessed their amazing progress over the next several months. They became very skilled and highly motivated Infantrymen, Scouts, and Mortar men. They learned how to work together as part of a team, as a part of their unit. By late-summer of 1966, they were almost ready, and they were motivated for combat. Yet they were untested. The true test would come soon enough in Vietnam.

## Jon Palmer Selects Bill Comeau to be His RTO

At Fort Lewis, Bill Comeau was Alpha Company's RTO for the Third Platoon Leader from the time he began his Advanced Unit Training after his basic training. That was around April 1966 when the 4th ID soldiers began training with the old PRC- 10 radios. He carried the radio for Platoon Sergeant Eugene Barton for about two months before the new Third Platoon Leader, Lieutenant James Olafson, arrived fresh from Officer Candidate School in late May.

Bill remained in that RTO role until the day he boarded the troop ship for Vietnam on September 21st, 1966. On that day he was told to get his gear together and report to the Headquarters Section where then-First Lieutenant Palmer told him that he had chosen Bill to be his RTO. Bill had no idea why Lieutenant Palmer shed his earlier RTO in favor of Bill. He guessed that it was probably because Bill was very familiar with radio protocol and the phonetic alphabet and that is what swung the choice to him.

Bill later said it was very fortuitous for him because all the Platoon Leaders' RTOs became casualties during his

Vietnam tour of duty. The man who took Bill's place as the Third Platoon Leader's RTO, Larry Barton, was killed on the morning of the Battle of Suoi Tre. ₃

## The Final Departure

In late September of 1966 it was time for the $2^{nd}$ Battalion, $12^{th}$ Infantry to deploy to Vietnam with the $4^{th}$ID. First Lieutenant Jon Palmer and his Alpha Company, $2/12^{th}$ Infantry boarded the troop ship Nelson M. Walker for the long ride across the Pacific Ocean to Vietnam. They boarded the ship at the Port of Tacoma, Washington, travelled north through Puget Sound, viewing the beautiful Seattle city skyline as they sailed past Seattle.

The troops could see the iconic Seattle Space Needle standing tall in the distance. The ship turned west at the Strait of Juan De Fuca and headed out into the Pacific Ocean travelling southwest for the three-week journey to Vietnam. Little did they know that in exactly six months from the very day of their departure (September $21^{st}$, 1966), these battle-trained yet untested soldiers would be involved in one of the biggest one-day battles of the Vietnam War – The Battle of Suoi Tre.

# Chapter 8 – Background Prior to the Battle of Suoi Tre

## Overview to the Suoi Tre Battle

The following chapters describe the Battle of Suoi Tre events based on a compilation of several historical documents that described the battle from various different viewpoints.

### NVA Lessons from the Ia Drang Valley Battle

About the time the American veterans of the Battle of Suoi Tre received their draft notices (1965), North Vietnamese General Chu Huy Man, a Moscow-trained intelligence officer, learned a valuable lesson that would shape the events of the Suoi Tre battle. In October 1965 General Man was tasked with drawing American units into a battle in the Ia Drang Valley in the Central Highlands of South Vietnam in order to determine the Americans' combat capabilities. He did this by attacking the US Special Forces base at Plei Me in the Central Highlands of South Vietnam.

This attack elicited a US Army response which was to send the 1st and 2nd Battalions of the 7th Cavalry Regiment and the 2nd Battalion of the 5th Cavalry Regiment into the Ia Drang Valley in early November 1965, to locate and engage his North Vietnamese Army (NVA) units.

Despite having a significant numerical advantage, the NVA forces suffered a decisive defeat there due in large part to the effectiveness of the supporting American artillery units that provided accurate and devastatingly lethal supporting fires. [1]

That was the infamous Battle of the Ia Drang Valley led by Lieutenant Colonel Hal Moore. After suffering devasting losses in that battle, General Man was to share what he learned with the North Vietnamese National Liberation Front (NLF) commanders.

One lesson he believed he learned was, if given the choice to attack and defeat a major American unit, it is wise to choose an artillery base to attack. This conclusion by General Man set the stage for their overwhelming attack at Fire Support Base (FSB) GOLD during the Battle of Suoi Tre. [1]

## Suoi Tre Battle – Background

Late in 1966 US Army intelligence reports indicated that the enemy was planning a major attack on US forces originating from somewhere in the jungles north of Saigon. In response to these intelligence reports, US Commanders planned to conduct a major invasion into the enemy's base of operations believed to be located somewhere in the heavy jungles of War Zone C. The target of this major invasion was the headquarters of the enemy's Central Office for South Vietnam (COSVN). COSVN was the headquarters of the commanders who were directing all the enemy activity in the South Vietnamese theater for the NLF. [1]

On February 22nd, 1967, nearly three American divisions began setting up an offensive operation that swept through the heavy jungles of War Zone C from east to west. This invasion into War Zone C, called Operation Junction City, included the largest U.S. Army aerial invasion of this conflict. It consisted of 249 helicopters and a number of fixed wing aircraft. After three weeks, little was accomplished during this part of Operation Junction City. The enemy continued to hide in the jungle and was content to allow the American forces to locate many of their abandoned base areas and supply locations. Phase I of Operation Junction City ended on March 15th, 1967, but preparations were made to return to War Zone C after a brief rest and maintenance period. [1]

Phase II of Operation Junction City consisted of returning to War Zone C with 24 American battalions to continue to search the heavy jungles for the elusive enemy forces. The target was a suspected jungle area where the 272nd VC Regiment and the command headquarters of the NLF South Vietnam were believed to be located. A loose cordon was set around the target area of operations (AO) using the 173rd Airborne Brigade; the 2nd Brigade, 1st Infantry Division; and the 3rd Brigade, 4th Infantry Division which also established some fire support bases. All three brigades were to perform a thorough sweep of their areas of operation (AOs) while the 1st Brigade, 9th Infantry Division secured the Highway 13 supply route to the east. [1]

# March 18th - Three Days Prior to the Suoi Tre Battle

Phase II of Junction City began on 18 March 1967, when the commander of the 3d Brigade, 4th Division, Colonel Marshall B. Garth, sent a mechanized infantry battalion (the 2nd Battalion, 22nd Mechanized Infantry) from the Brigade Base Camp at Dau Tieng through the jungle to seize a clearing designated Landing Zone (LZ) SILVER, twenty-five kilometers north of the village of Dau Tieng.

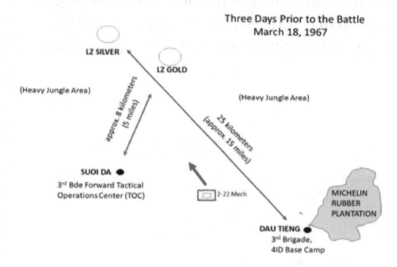

He intended to airlift from Dau Tieng on the following morning the remainder of his brigade, one artillery and two infantry battalions, into the clearing at LZ SILVER to establish a large firebase there, and then to sweep west toward Route 4. The operation did not go as planned. Slowed down in the jungle by mines and fire from RPG2s, the 2nd Battalion, 22nd Infantry mechanized force came upon an uncharted stream with banks so steep that the armored personnel carriers (APCs) were unable to cross. [2]

99

Also on Saturday, March 18ᵗʰ, 1967, Colonel Garth airlifted two of the three maneuver battalions from the 3ʳᵈ Brigade, 4ᵗʰ Infantry Division – the 2ⁿᵈ Battalion, 12ᵗʰ Infantry Regiment and the 3ʳᵈ Battalion, 22ⁿᵈ Infantry Regiment – by fixed-wing aircraft from the 3ʳᵈ Brigade Base Camp at Dau Tieng to their staging area at Suoi Da, located at the base of the Black Virgin Mountain near War Zone C. The third element — the 2ⁿᵈ Battalion, 22nd Mechanized Infantry — continued cross-country north into War Zone C with the task of securing a landing zone (designated LZ SILVER) to be used for the later insertion by helicopters of the two other light infantry battalions. ₂

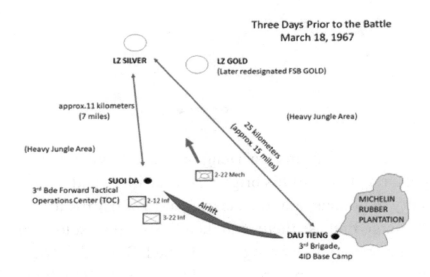

100

The plan was for Charlie Company, 3$^{rd}$ Battalion, 22$^{nd}$ Infantry to remain at Suoi Da during the subsequent air-insertion operation into LZ SILVER to provide security for the 3$^{rd}$ Brigade's staging area near Suoi Da.

Ultimately, the 2$^{nd}$ Battalion, 22nd Mechanized Infantry received continuous harassment fire and was unable to cross the stream to reach the original light infantry's landing zone (LZ SILVER) which was seven miles north of the jump off point northeast of Suoi Da. [1]

## March 19$^{th}$ - Two Days Prior to the Suoi Tre Battle

Rather than delay his main effort until the stream was forded by the 2/22$^{nd}$ Mechanized Infantry Battalion, Colonel Garth changed his plan. He directed the remainder of the brigade to an alternate, closer landing zone, designated LZ GOLD, on the morning of the nineteenth without providing any armored security forces at LZ GOLD to secure this Landing Zone. [1]

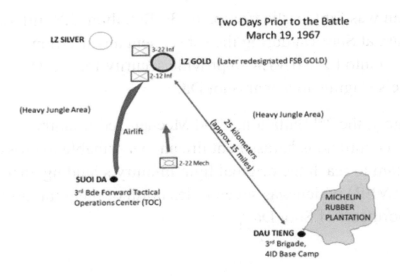

On Sunday, 19 March the 2nd Battalion, 12th Infantry loaded onto Bell UH-1 Iroquois (Huey) helicopters and was ready to fly into the alternate unsecured LZ GOLD. It was approximately 5 kilometers closer to the 3rd Brigade's advancing mechanized infantry battalion. Before the first lift departed, the decision was made to prep (bombard) LZ GOLD for an hour with US artillery fires. After the hour of prep fires, Bravo Company, 3rd Battalion, 22nd Infantry replaced the 2nd Battalion, 12th Infantry, and it airlifted into LZ Gold, followed by Alpha Company, 3rd Battalion, 22nd Infantry.

The first helicopter lift of troops into LZ GOLD was successful and uneventful. The second and third lifts, however, were attacked with command-detonated improvised explosive devices (IEDs) resulting in 15 American soldiers killed, 28 wounded, three helicopters destroyed, and three more seriously damaged. It was obvious that the enemy had been expecting the Americans to occupy this clearing. After a US soldier sweep of the area, the soldiers realized that the situation could have been much worse – they found an additional nineteen 82mm mortar rounds and two 175mm rockets rigged for remote detonation at the LZ. The 2nd Battalion, 12th Infantry subsequently airlifted into LZ GOLD without incident.

The 3rd Brigade forces finally secured the perimeter at LZ GOLD, re-designated as Fire Support Base (FSB) GOLD, at 1300 hours. The 3rd Brigade forces, now on heightened alert, spent a quiet night at FSB GOLD on March 19th. [1]


## March 20th - One Day Prior to the Suoi Tre Battle

The following morning at FSB GOLD, Alpha and Bravo Companies of 3rd Battalion, 22nd Infantry remained at the firebase to provide security and patrols in the local area. Meanwhile the 2nd Battalion, 12th Infantry including Alpha Company led by Captain Jon Palmer, with his RTO Bill Comeau went out on a sweep of the heavy jungle area to the west and northwest of the firebase.

To the southwest, two companies of the 2nd Battalion, 34th Armor Regiment along with its Battalion Command Group were sent to reinforce the 2nd Battalion, 22nd Mechanized

Infantry as it struggled to move northeast through the heavy jungle towards the firebase. [1]

Fire Support Base (FSB) Gold
March 20, 1967
One Day prior to the battle

Under the command of Lieutenant Colonel Raymond Stailey, the 2nd Battalion, 34th Armor moved northeast on March 20, 1967, as part of the 3rd Brigade, 4th Infantry Division Task Force commanded by Colonel Garth. Colonel Garth ordered the 2nd Battalion, 34th Armor to link up with the 2nd Battalion, 22nd Mechanized Infantry, commanded by Lieutenant Colonel Ralph Julian. Their mission was to continue their push together toward the Suoi Samat River to the northeast as a combined arms team. [3]

When these two mechanized battalion-sized units linked
up, they organized their combined forces into two separate
battalion-sized task forces. Each task force contained a
mixture of armored tanks and infantry APCs. Then these task
forces moved into positions along the edge of the Suoi Samat
River two kilometers southwest of Forward Support Base
(FSB) GOLD for the night. Earlier that afternoon, the scout
platoon of 2-22nd Mechanized Infantry had cleared a trail to
the north but had been unable to locate a ford or crossing site
across the river. [3]

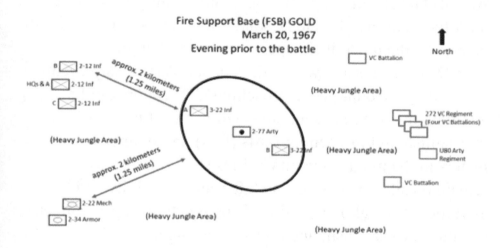

Further to the north, at dusk the 2nd Battalion, 12th Infantry
settled into their night-time jungle positions located near
the originally proposed LZ SILVER approximately two
kilometers to the northwest of FSB GOLD. Captain Palmer
instructed his Alpha Company troops to start preparing their

night defensive positions as he and his RTO Bill Comeau reported to their Battalion Commander to discuss the next day's actions. [1]

The day of 20 March was uneventful for all these units who were moving through the jungle: the 2nd Battalion, 12th Infantry; the 2nd Battalion, 34th Armor; and the 2nd Battalion, 22nd Mechanized Infantry. Although there were clear signs that the enemy had been in the area, the American soldiers found only abandoned enemy encampments as they made their way through the heavy jungle that day. [1]

At FSB GOLD, the 3rd Battalion, 22nd Infantry sent out at dusk two reinforced infantry squads to establish night ambush patrols on the most likely enemy avenues of approach to GOLD. Their mission was to disrupt and destroy any enemy forces they encountered approaching GOLD at night. In addition, the battalion sent out small teams of infantrymen to establish night Listening Posts (LPs) approximately 100 meters in the jungle beyond GOLD. Their mission was to remain on silent listening watch for enemy activity and to alert the 3rd Battalion by radio of any pending surprise attack should they hear suspicious activity during the night.

By the evening of 20 March, the clearing known as Fire Support Base GOLD contained a full Artillery Battalion and an Infantry Battalion at two-thirds of its full strength. The 2d Battalion of the 77th Artillery (105-mm, towed artillery guns) was commanded that day by the deputy commander, 25th Division Artillery, Lieutenant Colonel John W. Vessey. The 3rd Battalion of the 22nd Infantry, less one company, was under the command of Lieutenant Colonel John A. Bender. In all, about 450 men defended FSB GOLD. [1]

The plans for the next day were to conduct battalion sweeps to the northwest to locate a 30-to-40-man enemy force which Colonel Garth had previously spotted from his helicopter earlier that afternoon. [4]

On that evening of 20 March 1967, none of these 3rd Brigade forces were aware that the formidable 272nd VC Regiment was moving into attack positions in the nearby jungle areas to the North, East, and South around FSB GOLD. They were preparing to conduct a massive surprise attack on the following day to annihilate the 3rd Brigade of the 4th Infantry Division.

# Chapter 9 - The Battle of Suoi Tre, March 21, 1967

## 0429 hours - At FSB GOLD:

At 0429 hours on 21 March an ambush patrol from Bravo Company, 3rd/22nd Infantry reported movement in the jungle to the East beyond GOLD. Shortly after that, the jungle fell silent, and no more movement was reported.

## 0630 hours - At FSB GOLD:

At 0630 hours, as the patrol was preparing to move back to GOLD, they spotted two enemy soldiers and engaged them with grenades and small arms. A major firefight ensued. Captain Walt Shugart, Commander of Bravo Company, 3rd/22nd Infantry, began to organize a squad to move out to support the troops in contact. Before they could leave the perimeter wire, however, the sound of enemy mortar rounds leaving tubes rang out from the surrounding jungle. FSB GOLD began receiving heavy mortar fire around the perimeter and at the artillery emplacements. Lieutenant Colonel John A. Bender, the Battalion Commander of 3rd/22nd Infantry, notified Colonel Marshall B. Garth, the Brigade Commander, and the Brigade Tactical Operations Center (TOC) at Suoi Da that GOLD was under attack. [1]

Meanwhile his infantrymen scrambled into their holes while the base howitzers placed high-angle fire on the suspected mortar sites. Artillery guns at two nearby US firebases also

provided supporting fires, laying down protective barrages all
around GOLD. <sub>2</sub>

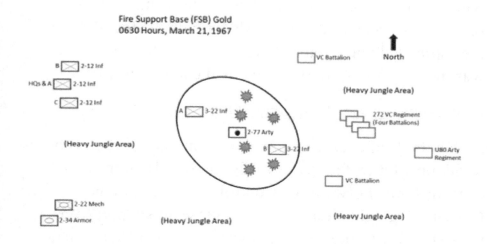

Fire Support Base (FSB) Gold
0630 Hours, March 21, 1967

Private First Class (PFC) Lawrence E. Melass of Freeport and
Lake Jackson, Texas was trying to grab a few extra minutes
of sleep. Specialist 4th Class (Sp4) Gary L. Coburn, 20, of
Redding Ohio, wasn't as fortunate. He had to be up early, to
begin brewing coffee for the 220 men of the 2d battalion, 77th
Artillery Regiment, assigned to the 4th infantry division. A
few yards away, Sp4 Raymond Riha, 21, of a Chicago suburb
was bent over a helmet of cold water, gazing at his lathered
face. He picked up his safety razor. Behind them, an explosion
broke the morning stillness. Then another, and another. Each
was closer than the last. His face still covered with shaving
cream, Riha grabbed his rifle and dashed for cover. Coburn
dropped his pots, picked up his rifle, and darted into a bunker.
The first explosion rolled Melass from his sack. Someone

screamed, "medic, medic!" Larry Melass found his medical bag and dashed outside, into a hail of bullets. One United States sergeant who had been quietly sipping black coffee when the first mortar hit would never know it. When Melass reached the scene of the first calls for help, he found three men sprawled out together. Two were still alive. The other was the sergeant. A mortar round had cut him in two. [3]

## 0630 hours - at the 3rd Brigade TOC:

As hundreds of enemy 61mm and 82mm mortar rounds began to fall on GOLD, the Brigade TOC at Suoi Da immediately sent Air Force Forward Air Controllers (FACs) in their O-1 Birddog light aircraft to direct close air support over GOLD. US Air Force F4 Phantoms from Bien Hoa Airfield were alerted and scrambled to provide that support. Colonel Garth, the 3rd Brigade Commander, commandeered the only available aircraft, an OH-23 bubble helicopter, to direct the battle from above. [1]

## 0635 hours - at FSB GOLD:

The Viet Cong (VC) were preparing for an all-out assault to overrun the base, leaving no survivors, just as they had done against the Army of the Republic of Vietnam (ARVN) units in the past. The attacking force was comprised of the four battalions of the 272nd VC Regiment reinforced with two additional infantry battalions and supported by the U80 Artillery Regiment. In total, 2,500 enemy troops were committed to the assault on the 450 defenders of GOLD. [1]

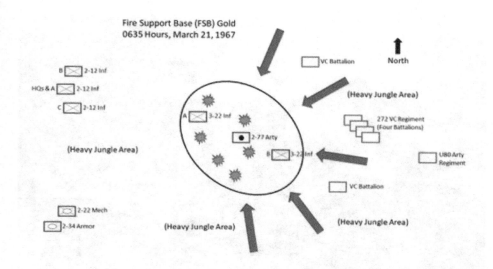

Fire Support Base (FSB) Gold
0635 Hours, March 21, 1967

At 0635 hours the concentration of the enemy mortar barrage shifted onto Alpha Company, 3rd/22nd Infantry at the western side of GOLD. This initiated a VC ground assault on Bravo Company along the eastern side. By 0638 hours, all Bravo Company platoons were reporting enemy inside the wire. Soldiers with 1st Platoon reported hand-to-hand combat along their portion of the southeastern corner. The battle was quickly getting out of control. At 0640 hours Colonel Garth alerted the nearby battalions in the jungle to prepare for a hasty movement through the jungle to reinforce GOLD. ₁

The 2nd/77th Artillery Battalion, consisting of three artillery batteries, was positioned in the center of GOLD. This battalion was commanded by Lieutenant Colonel John Vessey.

Artilleryman Sergeant James W. Evans (Buffalo, NY) was working as a gunner for the 2nd Battalion, 77th Artillery at GOLD when the battle started.

According to Sergeant Evans, mortars were falling everywhere, and soon enemy soldiers began running towards the American bunkers in screaming "human waves". The American soldiers began to fight for their lives.

Sergeant Evans, a 26-year-old gunner from Battery A, was picked to work as a rapid reactionary force member to drive the advancing enemy back away from the hard-hit perimeter. His M-14 jammed, and he had to work the bolt by hand as he fired into the never-ending ranks of Viet Cong. 4

## 0655 hours - at 2nd/12th Infantry Battalion in the jungle:

By 0655 hours the 2nd/12th Infantry Battalion was preparing to move out to reinforce GOLD per Colonel Garth's orders. Five minutes later, three of the four companies of the 2nd/12th Infantry received incoming artillery fire which wounded 13 and killed one soldier.

The Battalion Commander, Lieutenant Colonel Joe Elliot, was among the wounded. Charlie Company, 2nd/12th Infantry did not receive casualties from the incoming artillery fire because it was some distance away from the other companies of the battalion.

Charlie Company was directed to move southeast toward GOLD shortly after the incoming artillery barrage. ₁

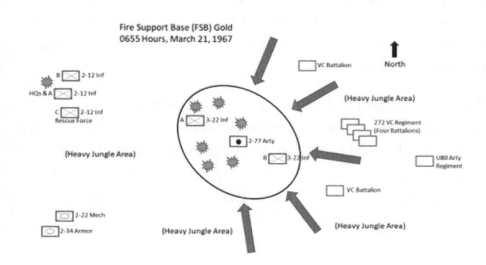

## 0655 hours - at 2nd/22nd Infantry Battalion & 2nd/34th Armor Battalion:

Meanwhile, the mechanized units located in the jungle two kilometers to the south were blocked by the Suoi Samat River. The 2nd /22nd Mechanized Infantry Task Force and the 2nd/34th Armor Task Force had no way to move their tracked vehicles across the river. Scouts were sent to search for a suitable crossing while the situation at GOLD worsened. [5]

At 0700 hours, incoming mortar fire landed among the 2nd/34th Armor Task Force's tank positions. Although ineffective, the mortar fire caused the tanks to disperse to get out of the impact area.

Straddling each other's tracks to clear a path wide enough for the tanks, the M113s pushed forward as fast as the jungle growth allowed. The smell of diesel smoke filled the air as the two battalion task forces crashed through the underbrush. The mortar fire gradually tapered off, with no casualties or vehicle damage reported.

Although initial progress along the trail went well, maintaining dispersion and getting all the vehicles to converge on the fording site proved time-consuming. Colonel Garth, anxious to get a relief column to the fire base, radioed, "If a vehicle throws a track, leave it. Let's get in there and relieve the force!" [5]

114

## 0700 hours – at FSB GOLD:

By 0700 hours the small US force at GOLD was engaged in a bitter, hand-to-hand struggle with the enemy. The situation inside GOLD had become by 0700 hours so critical that the US artillery guns within the perimeter were lowered to fire directly into the waves of advancing enemy soldiers with high explosive artillery rounds.

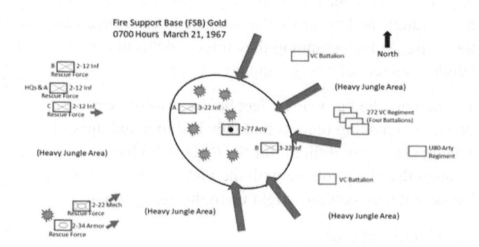

## 0715 hours - at 2ⁿᵈ/12ᵗʰ Infantry Battalion in the jungle:

Captain Palmer's Alpha Company moved out 15 minutes after Charlie Company to reinforce GOLD after tending to their wounded. The battalion command section, including the wounded Lieutenant Colonel Elliot, traveled to GOLD as part of Captain Palmer's group. A portion of Bravo Company remained behind to secure the landing zone for the medical evacuation (MEDEVAC). [6]

As Captain Palmer's Alpha Company led the way through the heavy jungle towards GOLD, Captain Palmer kept mentioning to his RTO Bill Comeau that he expected to cross the Suoi Samat River and was surprised that they never saw it. It was the dry season and when they came up on it all they saw was a dry gully, hardly a worthy landmark. [6]

Alpha Company moved as quickly as possible through the heavy jungle and never used a machete to clear their paths to the battle. At the beginning they travelled through a couple of hundred meters of heavy bamboo foliage.

The bamboo had grown six feet before it would curl downward making tunnels that they had to crawl through. That made it very difficult for the RTOs who had to maneuver through that thick foliage with the PRC 25 radios on their backs that kept getting caught up in the heavy vines. [6]

0715 hours - at FSB GOLD:

The first air support arrived around 0715 hours as the Forward Air Controller (FAC) in the 0-1 Birddog above guided four F4 Phantoms to the eastern tree line. Napalm was dropped from north to south first along the edge of the jungle to the east of GOLD, and then closer to the FSB where enemy troops were caught in the open.

By this time, enemy mortar fire was beginning to taper off largely due to the accurate counterfire from the US Artillery. Nevertheless, the advancing VC continued to attack the center of the FSB with accurate RPG fire and 57mm recoilless rifle fire from the wood line.

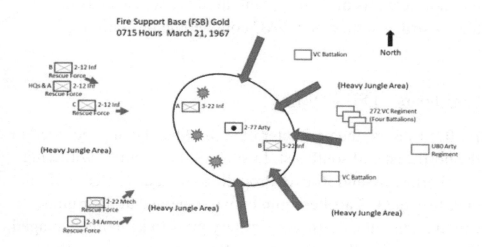

The acting commander of 2$^{nd}$ Battalion, 77$^{th}$ Field Artillery, Lieutenant Colonel John Vessey, moved to the artillery gunline to rally his artillerymen and organize a hasty repair of the damaged guns. Of the 17 damaged guns, the artillerymen repaired all but three of their guns during the battle. [6]

## 0745 hours – USAF Forward Air Controller Shot Down

At 0745 hours, the Forward Air Controller (FAC) plane was shot down by enemy heavy machine-gun fire and crashed into the trees beyond the fire base, killing both the pilot and observer. [5] According to Captain Shugart, "As it spiraled to earth the pilot calmly told LT Pacheco, Shugart's Artillery Officer, 'Well, I guess you'll have to get a new FAC.'" [6] As the ramifications of the loss sank in, there was a short lull in the air strikes until a new FAC could come on station. ₅

## 0751 hours – FSB GOLD:

By 0751 hours, the perimeter of GOLD had been penetrated in the northeast and southeast. In spite of the enemy's withering small arms fire and Rocket Propelled Grenade (RPG) anti-tank fire, the US artillery gun crews remained at their guns, cannibalizing the destroyed artillery guns to keep the damaged ones firing directly at the enemy. Crew members from the destroyed guns stepped in to fill vacancies as US gun crew casualties occurred.

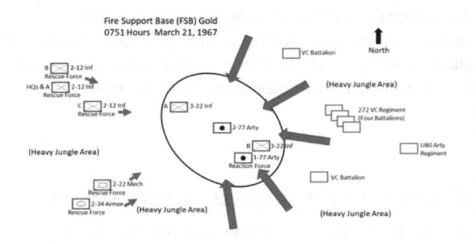

The Artillery Reaction Force, which had rehearsed their emergency reinforcement of the infantry the day prior, was alerted and assembled. [5]

All cooks, clerks, and other available personnel of the artillery battalion were formed into a reaction force that moved to block the enemy's penetration of the infantry's perimeter on the east side of the fire base.

Within minutes, the reaction force linked up with Bravo Company. Despite the best efforts of the artillery firing over the defenders' heads, the VC were in scattered foxholes. More importantly, ammunition was now in short supply. [5]

0815 hours – FSB GOLD:

By 0815 hours the northeast corner of GOLD had been completely overrun.

A wall of steel from supporting artillery pieces was fired within 35 meters of U.S. troops in the northeast and east area of the perimeter to turn back the swarms of charging black-clad VC.

Numerous times the VC were hit, would retreat to the protection of the nearby wooded area, and shortly would return bandaged up and ready for more action. [7]

Alpha Company, 3rd/22nd Infantry, which had been manning the western half of the FSB, sent reinforcements to its sister Bravo Company on the eastern half.

Minutes later a night ambush patrol from Alpha Company, 3rd/22nd Infantry which had been positioned two kilometers west of the FSB arrived at GOLD.

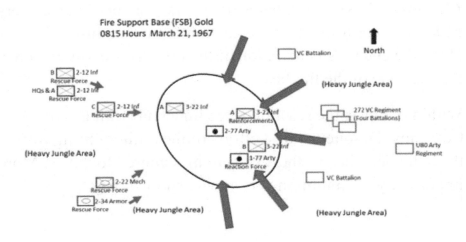

Fire Support Base (FSB) Gold
0815 Hours March 21, 1967

## 0815 hours – Flying above the Battle, the Brigade Commander:

Knowing that the men at GOLD could not hold out much longer, Colonel Garth checked the progress of the armor and mechanized units in the dense jungle to the south. When he learned that a suitable crossing had not yet been found, he ordered them to sink an armored personnel carrier (APC) in the Suoi Samat River and drive over it, if need be. Within a few short moments a crossing site across the river was located, and the armored-mechanized rescue forces sped across. Help was in route if the defenders at GOLD could just hold out.

<u>0815 hours - at FSB GOLD</u>:

The VC attack continued relentlessly.

Captain Shugart the Bravo Company, 3rd/22nd Infantry commander directed that 105mm artillery rounds, known as beehives, to be loaded immediately for direct fire into the advancing VC; the rounds had not been used previously because of their classified nature. Packed with thousands of small steel flechettes (small steel darts) in a single projectile, a beehive round could cut a wide swath in the enemy ranks. The Bravo Company commander decided to use the beehives in the 1st platoon sector first. After telling the platoon leader to get his men under cover, the commander instructed the artillerymen to lower the artillery guns and fire toward the advancing VC to the east and southeast. The effect was immediate. Although wide gaps had been blown in the attackers' ranks, more beehive rounds were requested along the whole eastern side. [5]

The flechette rounds initially quelled the advance, but more enemy VC continued to pour out of the wood line.

<u>0820 hours - at FSB GOLD</u>:

By 0820 hours the enemy advance became overwhelming.

Just then, another forward air controller arrived with several F-100 Super Sabres in tow. Air Force liaison officer MAJ Bobby J. Meyer, who was on the ground, recalled the result: "There must have been 500 of them (VC) coming at me, and this guy laid napalm right on top of them and then I didn't see them anymore." [6]

With the enemy troops still emerging from the wood line, Lieutenant Colonel Bender's northern sector began to crumble. [8] He gave the order for the eastern perimeter troops to fall back to secondary positions and make a last stand in front of the artillery. [5]

Bravo Company's forces began to move back into the fighting positions within the artillery perimeter.

Platoons began bounding back to their alternate positions in a move rehearsed the day prior. [5]

As Bravo Company pulled back Artilleryman Sergeant Evans, fighting with Bravo Company, grabbed a sandbag full of hand grenades, placed the bag in his teeth, put a grenade in each hand and started killing Viet Cong within five meters of his position. After Bravo Company had pulled back, Sergeant Evans found a new position with six Americans and began pouring small arms fire into the "human wave". [4]

During Bravo Company's retrograde back to the artillery's positions, a friendly M45 Quad-mount machine gun in Alpha Company's northern sector of the FSB was overrun by VC and turned towards U.S. forces.

Fortunately, the alert artillerymen reacted with one direct fire High Explosive (HE) artillery round, which eliminated the enemy threat before the enemy was able to fire the M45 Quad-mounted machinegun at the American troops.

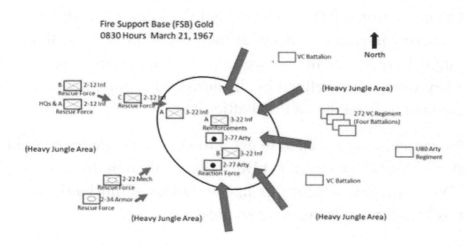

Fire Support Base (FSB) Gold
0830 Hours March 21, 1967

## 0830 hours - at the 2$^{nd}$/12$^{th}$ Infantry Battalion relief force enroute:

Around 0830 hours, from his helicopter Colonel Garth ordered Captain Palmer's Alpha Company and Headquarters of the 2$^{nd}$/12$^{th}$ Infantry Battalion to stop in place immediately.

On the radio, he asked Captain Palmer, the Alpha Company Commander, if they were anywhere near the jungle trail that ran from their earlier position toward the north of the clearing where GOLD was located. After a quick check on his map, Captain Palmer replied "negative".

Colonel Garth responded, "Good, I spotted a platoon of VC laying on the side of that trail waiting to ambush any relief column coming down. Start up your column and head to the battle. I'll deal with that ambush group with gunships." [6]

Captain Palmer, RTO Comeau, and the soldiers of Alpha Company moved as quickly as they could through the thick jungle to reinforce the beleaguered men at the fire base. They were overwhelmed by the horrendous noise that was emanating from the GOLD battle site.

No compass was needed to get through the jungle to the fight two kilometers away. RTO Bill Comeau thought to himself, "Wow, imagine what it was like on D-Day if this battle is producing such devastating sounds." [6]


### 0840 hours - at FSB GOLD:

By 0840 hours, Bravo Company, 3rd/22nd Infantry had completed its movement back to its secondary defensive positions. This opened up more friendly avenues of attack allowing for more beehive rounds to be used on the enemy who were quickly closing in on hand-grenade range. [3] The artillerymen lowered their artillery guns and fired at point-blank range making the beehives even more effective.

It was now over two hours since the Viet Cong attacked. The men wondered how many minutes they had left. Ammunition was running low. The VC were getting closer. Some positions had been overrun. [3]

In spite of a severe ammunition shortage, the 3rd/22nd Infantry's secondary defensive positions were still holding together.

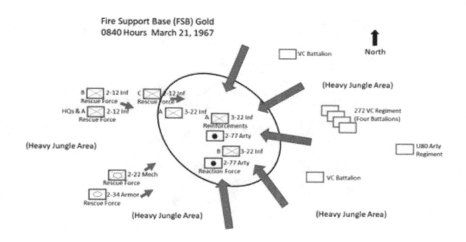

Fire Support Base (FSB) Gold
0840 Hours March 21, 1967

## 0845 hours - at the 2nd/12th Infantry Battalion in the jungle:

Minutes later, Captain Napper's Charlie Company, 2nd/12th
Infantry Battalion broke through the dense jungle and arrived
in the open area at the northwest corner of the FSB just
as the F4 Phantoms made another Napalm run along the
eastern wood line. Charlie Company moved in quickly to
reinforce Captain Shugart's northeast sector of GOLD. [4]
The infantrymen and artilleryman held their positions and
continued to fight from their retrograde perimeter until the
armored personnel carriers from the 2nd Battalion, 22nd
Infantry Task Force could hopefully reinforce them. 7

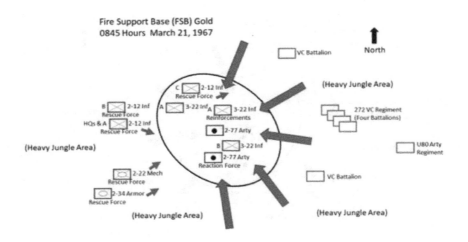

Fire Support Base (FSB) Gold
0845 Hours March 21, 1967

## 0845 hours - 2nd/22nd Mechanized Infantry and 2nd/34th Armor still in the Jungle

Meanwhile, alarmed by the radio reports at GOLD, the tank/infantry mechanized task forces moved with all possible speed through the heavy vegetation in its attempt to relieve the base. Although sporadic sniper fire hampered their movement, they made progress.

A new forward air controller arrived back on station at 0845 hours and coordinated more airstrikes. Helicopter gunships had also been called in to assist the defenders. CH-47 Chinook helicopters dropped fresh supplies of ammunition directly into the firebase. [5]

From his vantage point above the battlefield, Lieutenant Colonel Stailey, Battalion Commander of the 2nd Battalion, 34th Armor Task Force, helped to direct his battalion's lead elements to the river from his helicopter.

126

Calling forward his Armored Vehicle Launch Bridge (AVLB) and an M113 APC from the headquarters section, he put his contingency plan into effect. The APC was driven to the middle of the riverbed to act as an abutment. Once the crew was clear of their M113, the AVLB scissor bridge was set in, finally spanning the river. [5]

<u>0845 hours – at FSB GOLD:</u>

As the mechanized Task Forces closed on the fording site, air strikes were placed within 100 meters of GOLD. Napalm was burning up the foliage around the positions that enemy troops were using for concealment. Indirect artillery fire to hit the VC still emerging from the jungle was put on hold because of the aircraft in the area. [5]

The situation at the fire base had gotten worse. VC soldiers continued to pour from the woods from the north and east. Unknown to the VC troops, the 2nd/22nd Mechanized Infantry and 2nd/34th Armor Task Forces were consolidating in the wood line preparing to assault. The plan called for Charlie Company, 2nd/22nd Mechanized Infantry to attack northeast through GOLD and then swing north. The task force main body would skirt the wood line moving east and emerge swinging north, immediately spreading out to have room for fire and movement. They would continue along the wood line destroying all enemy forces in order to secure the eastern perimeter and prepare for an enemy counterattack. As the end of the column moved up to within 50 meters of the wood line preparing to counterattack, the defenders at GOLD were in dire straits. [5]

## 0900 hours – FSB GOLD:

Along the Bravo Company, 3rd/22nd Infantry sector, many troops were down to one grenade and one or two magazines apiece. Some soldiers had run out of ammo completely. Small pockets of men, out of ammunition, had resorted to picking up and firing fallen enemy weapons left on the battlefield; some soldiers used entrenching tools as clubs in desperate battles for survival. [5]

Like a swarm of ants, the VC continued to advance on the defending troops. With beehive rounds expended, the artillerymen resorted to firing high explosive artillery rounds at point-blank range. Enemy troops were within hand grenade range of the command bunker and five meters of the 3rd/22nd Infantry Battalion Aid Station. Having borne the brunt of the enemy's repeated attacks, Bravo Company, 3rd/22nd Infantry was on the verge of being overrun. Alpha Company, under moderate pressure, still held its original positions, but in some places the VC were within 15 meters of their line. [5]

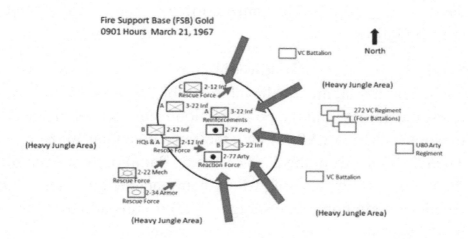

Fire Support Base (FSB) Gold
0901 Hours March 21, 1967

At 0901 hours, Captain Palmer's Alpha Company, 2nd/12th Infantry and his Battalion Command Group with the wounded Lieutenant Colonel Elliot burst through the western wood line and moved rapidly into FSB Gold to reinforce the beleaguered soldiers in Captain Shugart's Southeast sector.

The combined soldiers of Alpha Company, 2nd/12th Infantry, led by Captain Palmer with his RTO Bill Comeau, and Bravo Company, 3rd/22nd Infantry, led by Captain Walt Shugart, held their positions and were now preparing to launch a counterattack to the east to retake their original defensive positions. [1]

## 0912 hours – 2nd/22nd Mechanized Infantry and 2nd/34th Armor at FSB GOLD

Suddenly the VC attack slowed. In the distance, the troops could hear a roar, an unbelievable rumble. Across the charred trees, the gullies, and the pools of blood came armored personnel carriers (APCs) with their machine guns blazing. Then the tanks from the 2nd/34th Armor Battalion broke out of the jungle into the clearing firing their machine guns and their cannister main gun (huge shotgun-like) rounds into the mass of VC who were caught in the open ground. [3]

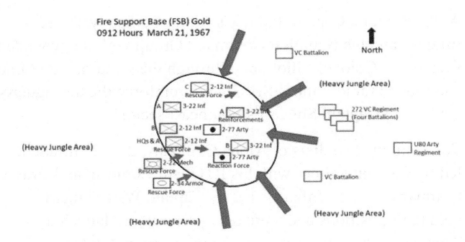

The APCs from Charlie Company, 2nd/22nd Mechanized Infantry Task Force, along with one platoon of 5 tanks, had broken through the jungle first and moved out of the southern wood line raking enemy with their machine-gun fire as they moved towards the southern tip of the FSB. Shortly after that, more APCs from the Recon Platoon of the 2nd/22nd Mechanized Infantry Task Force and tanks from 2nd/34th Armor Task Force moved out of the wood line sweeping south-to-north along the eastern side of the FSB. After clearing the southern end of the FSB, Charlie Company, 2nd/22nd Mechanized Infantry Battalion, with 5 attached tanks, turned north and cleared the eastern perimeter. [5]

With tank main gun canister rounds exploding among the VC troops in the open and machine guns blazing, the tanks and APCs began to fan out online, suddenly throwing the enemy off balance. Skirting the tree line toward the north, one tank crewman observed, "It was like shooting fish in a barrel". [5]

Stunned by the unexpected, armored onslaught, VC troops hesitated, unsure what to do next. The majority of enemy troops were caught in the open and were cut down by direct fire before they could reach the cover of the trees. A mechanic, aboard the Alpha Company, 2nd/34th Armor Battalion tank recovery vehicle, sat calmly on top of the vehicle, filming the action with his home movie camera while the rest of the crew threw grenades and fired their .50 cal. machine gun at the fleeing enemy. [5]

Responding to this new threat, groups of VC soldiers began to rush the vehicles but were quickly crushed by the rolling juggernaut. Others foolishly attempted to climb onto the tanks and had to be taken off with pistols, hand grenades, and even pioneer tools.

Anatol Kononenko, a 4.2 mortar forward observer with the 2nd/22nd Mechanized Infantry Task Force observed two tanks actually fire at each other using canister rounds to remove the enemy VC trying to climb upon their tanks. [5]

Some VC dashed for cover – and found none. The heavy vehicles advanced and rolled relentlessly over their bodies. Other VC grabbed at the vehicles and tried to climb up the sides. The American tanker soldiers aboard shot many of them at point blank range. [3]

**Battle of Suoi Tre – The Mechanized Counterattack in the final hours saved the beleaguered FSB soldiers and turned the Battle into a Decisive Victory**

With the VC on the run, artillery was immediately shifted farther east into the wood line in an attempt to kill as many enemy soldiers as possible with indirect fire. Charlie Company, 2nd/22nd Mechanized Infantry Task Force moving through the FSB, found a VC aid station just to the north of GOLD. [5]

Tying in with the 2nd/12th Infantry Battalion, the armored and mechanized vehicles quickly established a firing line outside the original perimeter and consolidated their combat power preparing for a possible enemy counterattack. [5]

Infantryman Bill Comeau, who was Captain Palmer's RTO, said the following: "2nd/12th Infantry was engaged as 2nd/22nd Mechanized Infantry passed through our ranks to engage the enemy that morning. We arrived at 9:02 and the Mech arrived at 9:12, ten minutes later. At the time of our entry into the clearing, the defenders were very near the point of exhausting the last of their ammunition. As we swept around to reinforce the defenders on the line it was apparent that they had no idea that anyone was coming to their aid. Needless to say, they were ecstatic. We were just as happy to see 2nd/22nd Mechanized Infantry come busting though the eastern tree line. If you read carefully the reports, the enemy by this time was in retreat. They saw us enter the fray and their scouts must have reported the arrival of the mechanized infantry and armor in the area and they felt the jig was up. Of course the 2nd/22nd Mechanized Infantry and 2nd/34th Armor caught them in the clearing. Believe me, it was a sight to see as they tore into their ranks. As they passed through our easterly forces, those men had to quickly move to get out of their way." [1]

The full US counterattack was underway with the reinforcing units and the surviving soldiers at GOLD.

Fighting with Bravo Company, Artilleryman Sergeant Evans drove forward behind the cover of the APC's and helped in knocking out small pockets of hiding VC. [4]

By this time, defeat was clear for the VC. Any remaining VC began to retreat towards the jungle. Captain Walt Shugart, Bravo Company, 3rd/22nd Infantry Battalion, ordered the counterattack along with Captain Palmer's Alpha Company, 2nd/12th Infantry Battalion. The two companies fired point blank into the VC caught inside the perimeter. They then moved east to the original Bravo Company, 3rd/22nd Infantry Battalion fighting positions. Meanwhile the 2nd/22nd Mechanized Infantry and 2nd/34th Armor Task Forces continued to pursue the retreating VC across the open areas and into the jungle northeast of the FSB.

Later the commander of the 2nd/22nd Mechanized Infantry Battalion, Lieutenant Colonel Ralph Julian said grimly "They weren't running when we came in, but when they saw what was coming, they ran." [3]

PFC Gary Lapp, of C Company, 2nd/34th Armor Battalion, was assigned as the loader on Tank C-25. Moving into the battle area, Lapp recalls the battle: "As the tanks were racing up and down the trails to get to Gold, I was down inside. The center of gravity on a tank is so high, that once it starts bucking back and forth, it is very difficult to stay up top in the loader's hatch with getting thrown around. Down inside I was having a hard time holding on to anything that would give me support. Sitting on the loader's seat with feet spread apart for directional support, my right hand was on the steel grid that protects the radios from the spent 90mm shell casings and my left hand was placed on the gun carriage. That was the best place to be. Once we broke through onto the LZ, SSG Badoyen told me to get ready. One of the prides I had in being a lowly loader, was that I knew how to keep the coax machine gun going, and I could load the main gun so fast it sounded like a semi-automatic. I remember racing across the opening for some distance before we opened fire. I also remember soldiers of the 77th Artillery, waving and cheering as we raced around them moving northeast. We had still not opened fire and were now in the clearing. I jumped up in the loader's hatch and I could see the back grill doors of three other tanks in front of us. Once I had jumped down inside to begin loading the main gun and keep the coax from jamming, I kept thinking: 'This is it, this is real combat. I wonder if an RPG will come through the front slope and kill us all? I hope SSG Badoyan has his pistol ready to keep anybody from jumping up on the tank and throwing a grenade inside.' I just kept loading that main gun and keeping the slack belts feeding into the coax. I recall the empty shell casings falling on the floor and using my boot to keep them away from the turret ring. When several shell casings stack up, they can roll into the drive gear and jam it up." [5]

135

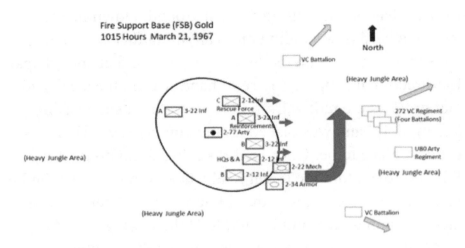

Fire Support Base (FSB) Gold
1015 Hours March 21, 1967

North

VC Battalion

(Heavy Jungle Area)

C 2-12 Inf
Rescue Force
A 3-22 Inf
A 3-22 Inf
Reinforcement
2-77 Arty

272 VC Regiment
(Four Battalions)

B 3-22 Inf

U80 Arty
Regiment

HQs & A 2-12 Inf

(Heavy Jungle Area)

2-22 Mech

B 2-12 Inf
2-34 Armor

(Heavy Jungle Area)

(Heavy Jungle Area)

VC Battalion

## 1015 hours – FSB GOLD: From the Ivy Leaf

By 10:15 hours the badly battered VC were hastily withdrawing to the northeast and southeast under attack by U.S. air strikes, artillery fire, infantrymen from the 2nd Battalion, 12th Infantry and armored mechanized vehicles of the division's 2nd/22nd Mechanized Infantry and the 2nd/34th Armor Task Forces. [7]

## 1045 hours – FSB GOLD:

The pursuing mechanized and dismounted infantry forces were eventually pulled back for fear of a possible ambush in the jungle. They returned to the FSB and began searching and collecting the enemy bodies.

Infantryman Jim Harden who was with the 2nd/22nd Mechanized Infantry Task Force told his own personal story of that day as follows:

"March 21, 1967 started like most. We went to 100% alert (Stand To) before dawn, then got ready for another day of patrolling. We had been doing this to the point that the days seemed to run together. As it got light I noticed there was an overcast, so maybe it wouldn't be too hot. Our squad was nearly at full strength, with 8 men and 2 Combat Engineers attached. These 2 fellows were great, they stood watches with us and helped out wherever they could. As we started to move out, we could hear a battle going on in the opposite direction. As we took position near the end of the column we couldn't find out any information as to what the battle was about. It didn't settle too well with the squad, to be driving away from a fight. Shortly the order came through to reverse direction and clear the trail so the two M48s could take the lead. While waiting, we found out that the 3rd/22nd was engaged at Fire Support Base GOLD and we were going to help them. By now the battle had been raging for a half hour, so we figured that it was going to be over by the time we got there, as we had done so many times before. The jungle was very heavy and the tanks were very slow. We got a message that the situation at FSB GOLD was critical and we were to bypass the tanks and make trail for them. Since we started at the rear, we were now near the front of the column. We moved around the tanks and formed a staggered column, widening the track as we pushed ahead. We ran at full throttle, clipping a few inches off the trees to widen the path for the tanks. Our V8 Chryslers were turning at redline in 2nd gear (20mph) and we were falling behind. We tried 3-4 range but after an initial burst of speed we would slow and have to drop back into 1-2 range. We had been told that slow or disabled PCs would be left behind. Our transmission was weak, but the driver (Willie) managed to keep us in the race. The jungle was getting thinner, and we could see light ahead. We took some small arms fire as we ran through the VC at the edge. We fired some to the flanks, but basically ignored the incoming and just swept on through. As we entered the clearing, I was struck by the sights before me. Artillery was pounding the flanks to the East, while at the same time I saw F-100s strafing the North side. In the middle of all of this, helicopter gunships were also strafing! Normally the Air Force won't come anywhere near supporting artillery and the gunships stay clear of close air support. Not today! A water trailer flew by, streaming water like smoke. We pulled to the far edge of the artillery positions and stopped online to dismount. I stopped the two Combat engineers and told them to stay on board and keep the .50 supplied. We had about 3,000 rounds of .50 but 600+ were in "spam cans". Spam cans were for quad 50s. They held 105 rounds, 5 too many to fit in a regular .50 ammo box. To compound the problem, the wrong end of the belt was on top! They had a key and opened like a can of spam, unless the tab broke, which it usually did. For a quad 50 the "wrong end" of the belt was started into the magazine and the belt cranked in to load it. We used a P38 can opener to open the bottom of them then topped off our regular ammo cans. I hit the ground, with my fire team on the left front of the PC. When Crum (our gunner) would fire, the muzzle blast rattled me so hard that I

138

couldn't see. I finally backed up till I was slightly behind him. I couldn't get low enough and decided that my ammo pouches were holding my posterior up too high. I unbuckled my web belt and pushed them to the side. With that part of my anatomy safe, I fired two 20 round magazines of grazing fire into the wood line. We were taking a lot of incoming, but I couldn't tell from where, nor did I know if any friendlies were in front of us. It was a gamble. A squad member ran over and flopped beside me. He wanted to know if my M16 had jammed. It hadn't and I had always claimed that a properly cleaned M16 would not jam. Little did they know how I despised that black piece of junk! He looked disappointed and told me his had. We laughed like two fools, while I got out my cleaning rod to clear the stuck case. It took several tries but we finally got it to fire a whole magazine without a jam. While doing this I noticed the two combat engineers popping up out of the cargo hatch with their M14s and firing. An artilleryman slid up beside me asking for 7.62 ammo. I apologized that all we had was linked. He didn't care, the choice was linked or none! The engineers threw out a case and off he went. He was back a minute later for grenades. Another case and off he went. There was a large, sandbagged position to my left, and I could see what looked like 10 men frantically de-linking the 7.62 belts and loading M14 magazines. As fast as they would fill a magazine, two fellows would pop up with M14 Autos and empty them! They also went through that case of grenades as fast as they could open them. Two of them started forward but one stopped and turned around when his sergeant demanded to know where he was going. He was explaining that there were still VC in a hole they had been trying to grenade. About then an RPD light machine gun peeked out of the ground and the soldier fell. I called for a medic who came with another man from the squad to our right. No questions asked, Doc and his 'guardian' took off. As they ran to the fallen artilleryman, Doc emptied his .45 into a dead(?) VC. His 'guardian' stopped and looked, then shook his head and caught up with Doc. While Doc worked on the man the 'guardian' crawled over to the hole where two VC were hiding, and in a reverse move, pointed his M16 into the hole like a pistol and emptied it. He pulled the RPD out and came back with Doc. He was excited with his souvenir that he wanted to take home and asked me what it was. I told him it was an RPD and I doubted that they would let him take it home. I asked Doc about the fellow he treated. He said he thought he would be OK, but the kid was recently married and worried about his wound, the bullet exited just above his family planning. As for the .45 shooting, Doc explained he was taking no chances! By now the rest of the PCs and tanks had caught up and were on line. I saw a blur come out of the woods and fly at one of the tanks. It bounce off the turret and sailed off into the woods to explode. The PCs started moving ahead on line. We got up to move alongside but the incoming was too heavy. Our squad and the one to the right of us were left behind. VC that were hiding in the many holes and folds of the ground started to get up and run. I laughed as one PC chased a VC. The .50 was firing away, but couldn't hit him as the PC bounded along. Finally the driver caught him. As the incoming fire dropped off, our two orphaned squads got online and moved forward. We came across pieces of a quad 50. It had been overrun and as the VC tried to turn it around, a 105 howitzer took it out! Doc's 'guardian' had stayed with a friend in my fire team, and as we paused in a small ditch, I heard a shout to my left followed by the 'thump' of an M79. I checked and found that a VC and come around a corner in the ditch and nearly bumped into these two. The 'guardian' pulled his trigger, only to find out he was empty and let out the shout. My grenadier turned and fired his M79. Too close to arm, the half pound 40mm took off the VC's arm and most of his right shoulder. We passed through the overrun positions of the 3/22, then turned left and started checking bodies. No one knew how to do that but we weren't taking blood pressure! We fixed bayonets and probed them. Finger on the trigger, safeties on Auto. We didn't run them through, just probed at sensitive spots to see if they flinched. At one point we came across a squad plus of VC, spread out evenly and on line. All were dead. We didn't look too closely but I guessed from the lack of apparent wounds, they had been cut down by a 105 beehive. I took an RPD from one and noticed that it was clean, oiled, and had never been fired. The squad leader spotted a 7.62 Tokarev pistol on one VC. He wanted it but was afraid of booby traps. I can't remember the sergeant's name, but he was a huge fellow with a Swedish name. He got the pistol out of the VC's hand, then took off running. When he reached the end of the lanyard the VC owner was snapped into the air like a puppy on a leash! We laughed till tears came. The PCs returned, Plt Sgt Kay was furious that we had stayed behind. We were furious that he had left us. He had called to mount up but we never got the word. My heart sank when I saw one of the combat engineers at the .50. Willie, the driver, wouldn't even look at me when I told him to drop the ramp.

The inside was a shamble of casings, links, empty ammo boxes, spam cans and personal gear that had gotten in the way. In the front on the bench seat was Crum, pale white and without a helmet. I called Doc over. He checked him out and filled out a evacuation tag while I got the story from the combat engineers. As they were clearing the area, Crum was reloading the .50 when he fell inside. His helmet had a bullet hole in the front, with an exit hole at the rear! Crum felt his head but found only a tiny scratch. He put on the helmet and went back to work. The bullet had traveled around between the helmet and the liner to exit at the rear. After firing another box or two through his .50, the full gravity of what could have happened sank in and he slumped inside in deep shock. Doc got him evacuated, while I started barking orders to the squad to cleanup the mess. They used entrenching tools to rake out the brass and links. A Chaplin from 3/22 came by, probably attracted by my NCO language, and thanked us for coming. I got an inventory of ammo, 300 rounds of .50 remained. That meant we went through 2,700 in less than a half hour!!! At that point we were called to reinforce recon platoon. They had gone out to recover the bodies from an L19 forward observer aircraft that was shot down during the battle. On the way they encounter the retreating VC who were still full of fight and took them on! That turned out to be a non-event but with only 300 rounds of .50 left, our pucker factor was way up there. When we got back to FSB Gold we found that the M88 VTR from the 2/34th Armor had scooped out a mass grave. We got to do police call. I don't know who did the body count or how they counted some of the pieces I threw in but 650 seems to be about right. I saw the weapons pile aside the grave and decided that this was the time to get a few pictures. I always sent my film to be developed, then home. Since they went home, I never took any "hamburger" pictures. This day was significant, so I would break my standing rule. I reached for my camera but it was gone! Both shirt pocket buttons were still buttoned but I managed to push the camera out when crawling around. It was inexpensive, but I hope someone found it and got some use from it. We formed a perimeter near the edge of woods for the night. We were winding down when we got a call to take cover, they were going to detonate an unexploded bomb. There was a boom and something big landed to our front. We reported it and a half hour later we got another Fire in the Hole. This time everything went black as the concussion swept over us. Not good for our rattled nerves. At dusk, I got tagged to take out the Listening Post. I wasn't too keen on that, we had heard that 3/22 had lost most of their LPs. I ended up with a reinforced squad, complete with an M60 and 800 rounds. We were all very edgy. As I chose a location, a trip flare went off behind us. One fellow started back toward the PCs. I got him stopped, but we gritted our teeth waiting for the .50s to open up. No one fired, even edgy they kept their wits. The VC didn't come back that night, but they sent their mosquitoes. Somehow we didn't have any insect repellant, so I passed around a can of weapons oil as a substitute. This is about all I can remember of that day." [9]

It had taken over two hours for the US relief forces to bust through the heavy jungle and arrive at the ongoing battle for GOLD. The relief forces arrived in the nick of time to counterattack and save the US troops at GOLD from being totally overrun and annihilated.

According to Lieutenant Colonel John Bender, the GOLD 3rd/22nd Battalion Commander, "It was just like the 10 o'clock late show on TV. The U.S. Cavalry came riding to the rescue." Lieutenant Colonel Bender was later awarded The Silver Star for his gallant leadership during this battle.

RTO Bill Comeau later said: "On a very personal note, I need to tell you about a friend that I made from the western defense perimeter. When the pursuit was taking place, I was standing at the southwest corner of the field. Out of the nearby A/2/12 bunkered positions popped a soldier of small proportions. To me he looked like a kid beginning high school. He trotted up to me and threw his arms around me. He kept repeating, 'Thank you, thank you.' Remember these men didn't even know that we were racing to save them from annihilation. They were overwhelmed. I told the 'kid' not to worry, we were here and this battle was over. I never forgot that man." Fifty-five years later, Bill reunited with that soldier at their A/2/12 Reunion, and they replicated that hug given on the battlefield 55 years ago. [6]

As RTO Bill Comeau and his fellow Alpha Company, 2nd/12th Infantry Battalion soldiers helped to police up the many dead Viet Cong soldiers lying about the field for burial, it became very apparent to him that this was an epic battle. It took 40 years for these 3<sup>rd</sup> Brigade soldiers to learn that this battle produced the largest enemy loss during any one-day battle to that date in the Vietnam war.

1145 hours – FSB GOLD:

By 1145 hours, the battle was pretty much over. The surviving VC who managed to make it back into the jungle had broken contact. Now there remained only the slow task of clearing the battlefield.

Treatment of the wounded and policing of the battlefield began. A platoon from Charlie Company, 2nd/22nd Infantry Battalion was sent out to locate the missing ambush patrol. They found that four of the men were dead, but one soldier had miraculously survived. Captured enemy soldiers and documents provided a wealth of information. [5]

Due to the large numbers of enemy dead, a mass grave was scooped out by one of the 2nd/34th Armor Battalion's M-88 recovery vehicles.

Surveying the devastation, the survivors at GOLD estimated that if the mechanized and armor units had arrived 15 minutes later, the VC would have overrun the base. [5]

The scope of the battle was so vast that five days later the security and ambush patrols from GOLD still found enemy weapons and bodies. They captured wounded enemy soldiers in the surrounding jungle up to a mile away.

By the battle's end Artillery Sergeant Evans had helped eight Americans to an evacuation site after they were found wounded. Sergeant Evans was an artilleryman who became an infantryman for six hours of this battle. [4]

Infantryman James D. Holder, from Alpha Company, 3rd/22nd Infantry Battalion, wrote about his admiration for the artillery in his story from the book, "War Stories – Utah Beach to Pleiku" by Robert O. Babcock:

"During the Battle of Suoi Tre, when we were informed that the enemy had penetrated our perimeter in three places, I watched the rear of our two-man position. As I stared out there looking for the enemy, I noticed that amid the 82mm and rifle fire, the artillery soldiers from 2-77 Field Artillery were standing in the open without cover, continuing to load and fire the 105mm howitzers with beehive rounds and HE into the tree line. I saw many of these fine soldiers hit the ground one at a time and then it hit me like a rock – these men were falling from wounds. I came away that day with a newfound pride in the artillery folks, which I have maintained to this day. We had cover, they did not, yet they stayed on duty continuing to fire their weapons until they were silenced or ran out of ammo. My hat is off to the men of the artillery." [10]

In just over five hours of intense fighting, the 3rd Brigade forces had secured the battlefield. They counted 647 enemy killed on the battlefield. It was estimated that the enemy carried away at least 200 more of their dead soldiers into the jungle. Ten wounded prisoners were captured.

One wounded VC prisoner was brought back to the Brigade TOC later that day. He was sitting on the ground alone, stripped down to his shorts with his hands tied. He had a steel fleshette dart sticking out of his rib cage. He appeared to be drugged and dazed. It was later believed that the VC attackers had been doped up with drugs prior to their attack to give them more courage during the attack. This explanation makes sense in view of the brazen human wave attacks they conducted that day.

The 3rd Brigade lost 33 courageous young American soldiers who were killed during that battle. 187 brave young soldiers were wounded, 92 of whom needed to be evacuated by helicopter to medical facilities. The remaining wounded US soldiers were treated on the scene and returned to duty at FSB GOLD.

Shortly after the battle, General William C. Westmoreland flew into the clearing by helicopter to congratulate the survivors. He stood up on the hood of an Army jeep to address the surviving soldiers and to praise them for their unrelenting spirit and bravery in the face of the overwhelming enemy threat that day. ₁

After General Westmoreland addressed the defenders of Fire Support Base GOLD, the 2/12th Infantry Battalion Commander, Lieutenant Colonel Joe Elliott, moved towards General Westmoreland to present himself to the General. As he approached, Westmoreland recognized his old Staff Officer and smiled.

Joe went right up to him and once in front of him, he raised his hand to salute. Joe had been bleeding quite a bit since he lost part of his thumb in the morning barrage and never completed his salute. He lost consciousness from the loss of blood and dropped at Westmoreland's feet. Joe was given first aid and carried to a dust-off chopper. He would spend the next two weeks in a Saigon hospital recovering from his wounds.[3] Lieutenant Colonel Joe Elliot was later awarded the Silver Star for Gallantry in Action at Suoi Tre. [6]

All participating units and soldiers in this battle were later awarded the Presidential Unit Citation by President Lyndon Johnson. General Westmoreland subsequently awarded The Distinguished Service Cross to Lieutenant Colonel John Vessey, the Artillery Battalion Commander at FSB GOLD, for his conspicuous bravery and leadership during this epic battle.

Lieutenant Colonel Vessey later rose to the rank of four-star General and became The Chairman of the Joint Chiefs of Staff under President Ronald Reagan.

It was reported that General Vessey went to Vietnam years later and spoke to the commander of the 272nd VC Regiment which attacked FSB GOLD that morning.

The Vietnamese commander told General Vessey that he wished the decision to attack GOLD could have been taken back.

The 272nd VC Regiment were destroyed as a fighting force for months after the engagement. [1]

The VC Leaders at Suoi Tre had made a big mistake in their assessments of these young American troops. According to one US Intelligence expert: "They were aware that the unit that they would attack was a recently deployed unit that had been in country for only six months. In addition, they knew that the bulk of the unit was made up of draftees. 'How tough could they be,' they asked. Actually, those soldiers were remarkable in their steadfastness.

With the proper leadership and outside support, they became an unsurmountable obstacle to the 9th VC Division's plans to annihilate an American unit and achieve a significant victory that may have tipped the balance of the war in the NLF's favor." [6]

As young Infantrymen, these 3rd Brigade, 4th Infantry Division soldiers, who were mostly Civilian Draftees, could not have possibly known that a historical battle had taken place on that day. This was their first "major" battle since their arrival in Vietnam, and they had nothing to compare it to. As civilian draftees, they found themselves in a place where they did not want to be, and yet they fought as professional soldiers with great courage and determination for themselves and for their fellow soldiers.

Although all of the participating units and soldiers in the battle were later awarded the Presidential Unit Citation (PUC), most of the soldiers in Captain Jon Palmer's Alpha Company, 2nd/12th Infantry Battalion didn't learn of the PUC award until later when they formed a veteran's group. Bill Comeau, the Alpha Company RTO, later informed them of it in his association newsletter. The PUC was not awarded until July

1968, seven months after these draftee soldiers returned to their homes, factories, farms, and offices when their 24-month induction service was completed. [1]

These brave American soldiers were just young kids at the time of this battle, yet they had now become battle-tested veterans much like the Greatest Generation who preceded them.

The amazing sacrifices of the young American soldiers of the Vietnam era cannot be overstated. America's Vietnam Veterans, now aging and deceased, have become to many Americans another example of the Greatest Generation.

# Chapter 10 - Aftermath

A few months after the battle of Suoi Tre, Captain Jon Palmer was about to complete his Vietnam tour of duty as an Infantry Company Commander. He had been notified that he was due for a reassignment to another much safer staff job.

On his final day as the Alpha Company Commander of the 2nd Battalion, 12th Infantry Regiment, Captain Jon Palmer called into his office his trusted RTO, Specialist 4th Class Bill Comeau, for a final farewell and quiet moment of time together.

At that time Jon Palmer informed Infantryman Bill Comeau that he was recommending him for award of The Bronze Star Medal for his outstanding performance in combat. [1]

Being a civilian Draftee Soldier with less than two years of Army service, Bill did not know or understand what this medal was or know its significance.

In a moment of light-hearted jest, Bill asked if he could trade the medal in for a reassignment to a safer job in Saigon.

Captain Palmer smiled at the notion and with a twinkle in his eye said, "Get the hell out of my office."

Infantryman Bill Comeau was later awarded The Bronze Star Medal. [1] He had previously been awarded the coveted Combat Infantryman's Badge for sustained performance as an Infantryman in combat.

Bill Comeau recalls the day he was awarded The Bronze Star Medal: "On the day before I left Vietnam, Larry Walter and I were ordered to report to the 2/12th Headquarters where we received our Bronze Stars from then 2/12th Commander, LTC James F. Greer. At that ceremony, A/2/12's former First Sergeant Sydney Springer made a special trip from Cu Chi, where he was serving as a Battalion Command Sergeant Major, to attend the ceremony.

"When I was pinned I looked over at him and he was smiling ear to ear. As he watched he winked at me. I didn't understand the significance of that day, but Springer certainly did. That was one of the most iconic moments in my life and had to keep it to myself for decades." [1]

Infantryman Bill Comeau remained in his position as RTO for two subsequent Alpha Company Commanders during the remainder of his tour in Vietnam. As an Infantryman and RTO, he survived an amazing 12 months of hazardous infantry combat duty in the jungle without being wounded or injured. He was lucky. At the end of his hazardous stressful Vietnam assignment, Bill rotated back to the "states" to Ft. Dix, N.J. where he remained for the final 3 months of his Army duty. He was processed out of the Army at Ft. Dix when he completed his two years of Army service as a Draftee Soldier. [1]

After his Army tour Bill returned to his hometown of New Bedford, MA where he still lives. He attended and graduated from East Coast Aviation Technical School in 1971 and served as a technician for over 40 years. William has a wife, two sons and a daughter. His son, Christopher, is a 21-year veteran of the US Air Force and is also a veteran, having served in Iraq during Operation Iraqi Freedom. [2]

In later years, Bill Comeau took on the extra duty as the unit historian of the 2$^{nd}$/12$^{th}$ Infantry Battalion in Vietnam, posting periodic 2$^{nd}$/12$^{th}$ Infantry Newsletters to the Vietnam Veterans who served together as a unit. He also arranged for and hosted several reunions for the 2$^{nd}$/12$^{th}$ Infantry, bringing together the Vietnam Veterans of that unit to maintain and preserve the memories and camaraderie of that special band of brothers.

When Captain Jon Palmer's Vietnam tour of duty was completed, he returned for a new stateside Army assignment. He received an early promotion to the rank of Major, and then returned to Vietnam for a second tour of duty. Jon Palmer continued his career in the Army and retired from the Army as a Lieutenant Colonel after 20 years of service.

During his career as an Infantry Soldier, Jon Palmer was awarded The Legion of Merit, The Bronze Star Medal for Valor in combat, 4 additional awards of The Bronze Star Medal for outstanding performance in combat, The Purple Heart for wounds received in combat, The Combat Infantryman's Badge, and several other awards for outstanding performance.

# Epilogue

One might ask why these young two-year Draftee soldiers demonstrated so much grit, perseverance, and bravery under severe combat conditions? Obviously, they did not volunteer for military service. They did not ask to be soldiers. They did not want to fight a nasty war in the far-away hot and steamy jungles of Vietnam. Yet these young soldiers did their duty admirably; these young kids performed in an outstanding manner for 12 long months under prolonged, miserable combat conditions. Why did they endure the misery of the Vietnam War and still perform so well?

Were they motivated by patriotism? Was it a sense of duty to their families back home? Was it their training and leadership? Was it the camaraderie and loyalty to their fellow soldiers? Was it all about personal survival? Was it something else?

Was it SPIZZERINCTUM? The Merriam-Webster Dictionary defines this word as: "The will to succeed." [1]

There is not a simple answer to the simple question of what motivated these young soldiers. No doubt there are many reasons why these young Draftee soldiers performed so well.

I asked Bill Comeau this question some 56 years after he completed his Vietnam service as a civilian Draftee. Here is some of what he said:

*"... we had a keen sense of pride for what we were able to accomplish when we all stuck together. At our [young] age we had nothing to point to as a comparable achievement.*

154

"Outstanding leadership was essential to our completing our mission without suffering an undue number of casualties. Training? Probably not, as we learned soon after we arrived that that traditional infantry training didn't prepare us for what we experienced in Nam. Fire and maneuver? Are you crazy? Get down as low as you can, looking for nearby cover and see if you can pick up the location of your target. Then hit him with a sustained burst.

"We didn't fight for a flag. We fought for the man on the left, and man on the right.

"Captain Palmer... told his replacement when he was asked what he should know about the men in A/2/12 before he took over: ' they are a very good group of soldiers who respond well to orders.'

"Understand this. Everyone of these men would rather be anywhere else in the world than in Vietnam. That was a very accurate description of our feelings. The futility of the exercise had seeped in by then. We knew what casualties we were suffering, yet after most skirmishes the enemy dragged away their casualties. Pretty tough to focus on the big picture when the reality of what we saw didn't offer us much confidence that progress was being made.

"Then the despised Infusion arrived where they pulled many of our men and sent them all over the country to serve in other units to prevent units being completely stripped of men when their rotation date came up. That took away a lot of the glue that kept us going. From then on, our lives revolved around short time calendars. We had seen so much that it was difficult

155

*to consider [anything but] survival as the overwhelming
motivation later in our tours.*

*"In the Pentagon Papers they mentioned calling back most
of the veterans of the war in 1968 for a final big push. They
would have had a real struggle to get us back into the jungle.
We did our part. The attitude was that we had done our duty
when so many of the young men had figured out how to avoid
Vietnam.*

*"We only had each other, which made our reuniting thirty
years later so sweet. Only three of our comrades committed
suicide before we could get to them. Who knows how many
we saved once we formed Alpha Association, and they had a
forum where they could vent all that anguish. [2]*

# Appendix A - The Presidential Unit Citation [1]

The 3rd Brigade of the 4th Infantry Division was awarded the Presidential Unit Citation for its actions at the Battle of Suoi Tre on March 21st, 1967

The text of the Presidential Unit Citation is as follows:

Award of the Presidential Unit Citation (Army) by The President of the United States of America to the following unit of the Armed Forces of the United States is confirmed in accordance with paragraph 194, AR 672-5-1. The text of the citation, signed by President Lyndon B. Johnson on 23 September 1968, reads as follows:

BY VIRTUE of the authority vested in me as President of the United States and as Commander-in-Chief of the Armed Forces of the United States I have today awarded

THE PRESIDENTIAL UNIT CITATION (ARMY) FOR EXTRAORDINARY HEROISM

TO THE FOLLOWING UNITS OF 3D BRIGADE, 4TH INFANTRY DIVISION:

BRIGADE COMMAND AND CONTROL PARTY

# AT FSB GOLD 3D BATTALION (LESS COMPANY C), 22D INFANTRY, 2D BATTALION (LESS COMPANY B), 34TH ARMOR, 2D BATTALION, 77TH ARTILLERY, 2D BATTALION, 22D INFANTRY, 2D BATTALION, 12TH INFANTRY

The 3rd Brigade, 4th Infantry Division and the attached and assigned units distinguished themselves by extraordinary heroism while engaged in military operations on 21 March 1967 in Suoi Tre, Republic of Vietnam. During the early morning hours, the Viet Cong 272nd Main Force Regiment, reinforced, launched a massive and determined ground attack and overran elements of the 3rd Battalion, 22nd Infantry and 2nd Battalion, 77th Artillery, located at Fire Support Base Gold near Suoi Tre, Republic of Vietnam. As the enemy penetrated the perimeter, the American troops set up an interim perimeter and continued to fire on the enemy. When the Viet Cong directed anti-tank fire upon the artillery position, heroic gun crews repaired their damaged guns and, at several points, fired directly into the advancing enemy. While the battle continued to rage and grow in intensity, the Brigade Commander was directing the 2nd Battalions of the 12th Infantry, the 22nd Infantry

(Mechanized), and the 34th Armor, to the besieged fire support base. At the same time, the support and service elements of the brigade began a furious aerial resupply of ammunition and medical supplies from the brigade rear base camp at Dau Tieng. As the 2nd Battalion, 12th Infantry, began its overland move to the fire support base, a heavy concentration of enemy mortar fire was directed upon their positions. Concurrently, mechanized and armor elements began moving across the Suoi Samat River at a ford which had only recently been located and which previously had been thought impassable. The mechanized unit, followed by the armor battalion, drove into the western sector of the engaged perimeter passing through engaged elements of the 2nd Battalion, 12th Infantry. Striking the Viet Cong on the flank, the 2nd Battalion, 22nd Infantry, smashed through the enemy with such intensity and ferocity that the enemy attack faltered and broke. As the fleeing and now shattered enemy force retreated to the northeast, the 2nd Battalion, 34th Armor, swept the position, destroying large numbers of Viet Cong. Throughout the battle, fighters of the United States Air Force, directed by the brigade's forward air controllers, provided close support to the fire support base and hammered enemy concentrations outside the perimeter. As the Forward Air Controller aircraft dived through heavy anti-aircraft fire to mark enemy positions, the plane was hit by ground fire, and crashed. After securing the fire support base, a sweep of the area was conducted, revealing a total of 647 Viet Cong bodies and 10 enemy captured. It is estimated that an additional 200 enemy were killed as a result of the aerial and artillery bombardments. Friendly casualties were extremely light, resulting in only 33 killed and 187 wounded. Through their fortitude and determination, the personnel of the 3rd Brigade, 4th Infantry Division, and attached units were able in great measure to cripple a large Viet Cong force. Their devotion to duty and extraordinary heroism reflect distinct credit upon themselves and the Armed Forces of the United States.

LYNDON B. JOHNSON

# Appendix B - More About Bill Comeau

To read a more detailed description of the Battle of Suoi Tre, one can read Bill Comeau's excellent book "Duel with the Dragon at the Battle of Suoi Tre," available on Amazon.

After the war, Bill Comeau returned to New Bedford and spent a quiet life working mainly as a technician in a local book manufacturing establishment. The war was behind him, and he spoke little of his time in Vietnam.

That all changed in the year 2000, when Bill and a few other Company brothers he served with in Vietnam found each other on the internet. They began Alpha Association, a veterans' organization of men who served with him in A Company, 2nd Battalion, 12th Infantry of the 4th Infantry Division.

Bill served as President, Newsletter Publisher, Historian and Website Manager from its inception. Within two years Bill and his wife, Chris, made several trips to the National Archives in College Park MD to research his company and battalion's history in Vietnam. It was important to have the ability to learn exactly what they accomplished in Vietnam. Actually, they accomplished a great deal in the time

that they served together. He was able to document the entire period beginning at the time they first formed as a basic training unit in January 1966 through the Tet Offensive period, when his company replacements were sent south to villages north of Saigon which were serving as a staging area for attacks on Saigon.

During those several journeys to the National Achieves, they collected everything that they had on not only his battalion, but the regiment dating back to its origin under John Adams in 1798. Even the Center for Military History did not have the original organizational data.

He also had everything on the formation of the original 4th ID during WWI. This information formed the basis for what was published in his quarterly newsletters, 'Alpha's Pride'. All that history was published and shared with the US Army Heritage and Education which continues to archive those newsletters to this day. There have been 93 issues, each containing at least 20 pages of stories. They serve as a source of living history for future historians.

In 2015, he organized the first Battle of Suoi Tre Event at Fort Carson where veterans of the battle could share their stories with the 2/12th Infantry and 2/77 Artillery soldiers who were serving in those units today. It was through these events that he got to meet, interview and befriend many of the principals of the battle. This allowed him to publish personal stories from the different units that performed so gallantly on that day. After that event he published a story on the battle that was published in the October 15th, 2015, Infantry Magazine, which serves the Infantry Leadership School at Fort Benning. Soon after that he was awarded the Order of Saint Maurice Medal, as a Legionnaire, to recognize him for his outstanding promotion of the United States Infantry.

Next, he was chosen as the Historian for the 12th Infantry Regiment Project. The project consisted of the construction of a monument honoring all those who served in the 12th Infantry. It was dedicated in April, 2017 at the Walk of Honor behind the US Infantry Museum at Fort Benning.

In September of 2022, his book, "Duel with the Dragon at the Battle of Suoi Tre" was published. It was the very first time that a complete story of his company and the units who fought in that historic battle were introduced to the public.

Bill continues serving the needs of his regional veterans as an Officer in both the Disabled American Veterans and a local VFW organization. He never lost his love for those veterans who served their country and who got little recognition by others who didn't understand the sacrifices that were made to keep our country safe and free. [1]

# Appendix C – More About Jon Palmer

This story describes some of Allyn Jon Palmer's experiences at West Point before he went to Vietnam, in addition to his Vietnam duty. To learn more background about Jon's time at West Point, one can read the excellent book titled "The Long Gray Line" by Rick Atkinson. This book depicts the experiences of the West Point Class of 1966 during the early-to-mid 1960's at West Point, and then it depicts their subsequent combat duty in Vietnam. Rick Atkinson's book also happens to describe the similar experiences of Jon Palmer's West Point Class of 1964 during the same timeframe. These similar West Point experiences occurred because Jon and his Class of 1964 were the West Point upperclassmen overseeing the first two years of the Class of 1966's experiences depicted in Rick Atkinson's book.

Jon's Class of 1964 were there during the tenures of Generals Westmoreland, Stillwell, and Davison; they were there to hear General MacArthur's famous "Duty, Honor, Country" speech in the Cadet Mess Hall; they were there during the inauguration and the assassination of President Kennedy; they were there to march in General MacArthur's funeral procession on that rainy, dreary day in New York City in April of 1964; they attended the Army-Air Force football game at Soldiers Field in Chicago and the celebrations that followed; they were there during President Kennedy's visit to West Point for the Class of 1963's graduation ceremony; Jon's classmates were the ones who helped instigate the Great Mess Hall Riot mentioned in Rick Atkinson's book; and they were there to hear William Faulkner lecture to the Class of 1964 during his visit to West Point.

Similarly, Jon's class suffered through Airborne and Ranger training together as a West Point class. In short, Jon and the Class of 1964 experienced the West Point education and training environments that existed during this early-to-mid 1960s period – the same environments that are depicted so well in Rick Atkinson's excellent book, "The Long Gray Line."

The same can be said for both classes' subsequent Vietnam combat experiences under General Westmoreland and later under General Abrams. Rick Atkinson's book describes, for example, the infamous Vietnam Battle for Hill 875 by the 173rd Airborne Brigade, during which four members of the Class of 1966 were killed in action. Also killed in that battle were two cherished members of Jon's Class of 1964: one was Jon's classmate Captain Mike Kiley, who was the A Company Commander; the other was his classmate, Captain Hal Kaufman, who was the C Company Commander. Both are mentioned in Rick Atkinson's book that describes this terrible battle. There were countless similar battlefield situations that the graduates from both classes faced in Vietnam.

The West Point Class of 1966 lost 30 classmates who were killed in action in Vietnam. Jon's Class of 1964 lost 24 classmates killed in action.

# About the Author

Douglas Barr served 20 years in the US Army as an Armored Cavalry officer. He served two combat tours of duty in the Vietnam War.

Initially he served as a Platoon Leader in the 4th Infantry Division with the 1st Squadron, 10th Armored Cavalry Regiment during their Vietnam training preparation at Ft. Lewis in 1965-66. This was the same timeframe described in this book. He then deployed to Vietnam in 1966 with the 4th ID and served there as the Troop Commander of "Charlie" Troop, 1/10th Cavalry Squadron during 1967. "Charlie' Troop was part of the 3rd Brigade, 4th Infantry Division.

During the Battle of Suoi Tre his "Charlie" Troop was the 3rd Brigade's reserve/reaction force. On the morning of the surprise attack, Captain Barr was at the 3rd Brigade's forward Tactical Operations Center (TOC). He monitored the Suoi Tre battle on the brigade's tactical operations network and experienced the actions taking place in and around the Brigade TOC during the battle. He later observed the horrific aftermath of the Suoi Tre Battle. This battle remained in his mind for over 55 years, until he met Bill Comeau. That meeting prompted him to write this story.

During his second Vietnam tour in 1969-70, he was assigned to the 2nd Brigade of the 1st Infantry Division (the Big Red One) as the Company Commander of "Bravo" Company, 2nd Battalion, 34th Armored Regiment.

# In Memory of Allyn Jon Palmer

While writing the final portions of this story, I learned the sad news that Allyn Jon Palmer had recently passed away at the age of 81 after a long illness. This struck me hard because I knew him - we had endured some difficult Army training together as young soldiers getting ready for war.

Allyn ("Jon") and I took Army Airborne and Ranger Training together at Ft Benning in late 1964. We underwent the grueling Ranger Training together in the same Ranger Squad. At that time those of us in Allyn's Ranger Squad referred to him as Allyn or Al.

For nine punishing weeks our 12-man Ranger Squad lived and trained together 24 - 7 in the mountains of Georgia and the swamps of Florida. All of us in that Ranger Squad endured tough times together as we learned how to be Army Rangers. For nine weeks we lived together in the mountains and swamps, we trained together, we patrolled the mountains and swamps day and night together, we ate C-Rations together when we could get them, and we slept during the few times we could.

Through it all, we learned that Allyn ("Jon") was a strong and reliable soldier whom we could depend upon - he always remained calm, deliberate, and confident during those stressful times.

From Ranger Training we both went to the 4th Infantry Division at Ft. Lewis, and later deployed together to Vietnam in separate units of the 4th ID. In Vietnam, the soldiers knew

Allyn Jon Palmer as a brave, wise, and confident leader during dangerous combat situations. His fellow soldiers respected him because he valued them and always watched out for them. They will always remember him in that way.

## Notes and References:

### Preface

1 – General of the Army Douglas MacArthur, DUTY-HONOR - COUNTRY, Rolton House Publishers, Inc., First Edition, Copywrite 1962, 26.

2 – Article by James Webb Jr., "Heros of the Vietnam Generation," The American Enterprise Institute, July/August 2000.

### Chapter 2

1 – William Comeau. Duel with the Dragon at the Battle of Suoi Tre, Deeds Publishing, First Edition, Copywrite 2022.

Note: William Comeau was a member of Alpha Co, 2nd/12th Infantry, 3rd Brigade, 4th ID, during the Battle of Suoi Tre.

### Chapter 3

1 – Newsletter, A/2nd/12th Infantry: 1966-67 "Alpha's Pride," Vol 12, Issue 2, October 1, 2011, by William Comeau,

Note: William Comeau is a Combat Veteran of Alpha Co, 2nd/12th Infantry, 3rd Brigade, 4th ID in Vietnam.

## Chapter 4

1 – "The Howitzer - West Point Class of 1964 Yearbook," 59.

2 – "The Howitzer - West Point Class of 1964 Yearbook," 75.

3 – General of the Army Douglas MacArthur, DUTY-HONOR - COUNTRY, Rolton House Publishers, Inc., First Edition, Copywrite 1962, 28.

## Chapter 5

1 – Newsletter, A/2nd/12th Infantry: 1966-67 "Alpha's Pride," Vol 12, Issue 2, October 1, 2011, by William Comeau,

## Chapter 6

1 – Newsletter, A/2nd/12th Infantry: 1966-67 "Alpha's Pride," Vol 12, Issue 2, October 1, 2011, by William Comeau,

2 – William Comeau. Duel with the Dragon at the Battle of Suoi Tre, Deeds Publishing, First Edition, Copywrite 2022.

## Chapter 7

1 – Newsletter, A/2nd/12th Infantry: 1966-67 "Alpha's Pride," Vol 12, Issue 2, October 1, 2011, by William Comeau.

2 – Robert O. Babcock, War Stories, Volume III: Vietnam 1966-1970, Deeds Publishing, Copywrite 2001, 2016, 2019, 23-24.

Note: Bob Babcock served as an Infantry Platoon Leader in Vietnam in 1966-67 with Bravo Co, 1st/22nd Infantry, 4th ID.

3 – Personal Story from William Comeau, Alpha Co, 2nd/12th Infantry, 4th ID.

## Chapter 8

1 – Infantry Magazine Article, Oct-Dec 2015: "The Battle of Suoi Tre," by William Comeau, and CPT Andrew Loflin.

2 – William Comeau. Duel with the Dragon at the Battle of Suoi Tre, Deeds Publishing, First Edition, Copywrite 2022.

3 – Armor Magazine Article, May-June 2000: "The Battle of Suoi Tre: Viet Cong Infantry Attack on a Fire Base Ends in Slaughter when Armor Arrives" by First Sergeant Christopher P. Worick

4 – Report from Bob Babcock, 4th Infantry Division Historian, to Commanders, Officers, NCO's and Soldiers of the 4th Infantry Division, 21 March, 2010.

# Chapter 9

1 – Infantry Magazine Article, Oct-Dec 2015: "The Battle of Suoi Tre," by William Comeau and CPT Andrew Loflin

2 - Report from Bob Babcock, 4th Infantry Division Historian, to Commanders, Officers, NCO's and Soldiers of the 4th Infantry Division, 21 March, 2010.

3 – Chicago Tribune Article: "Gallant Yanks Grab Rifles and Stop Savage Attack Shell Blasts Send them in Action, Some to Heroes' Deaths," March 23, 1967

4 – Article from Ivy Leaf News, April 7, 1967: "Artilleryman Turns Infantryman to Drive Back Charging Viet Cong", by SP4 Gary M. Silva

5 – Armor Magazine Article, May-June 2000: "The Battle of Suoi Tre: Viet Cong Infantry Attack on a Fire Base Ends in Slaughter when Armor Arrives" by First Sergeant Christopher P. Worick

6 – William Comeau. Duel with the Dragon at the Battle of Suoi Tre, Deeds Publishing, First Edition, Copywrite 2022.

7 – Article from Ivy Leaf News, March 24, 1967: "3rd BDE Kills 596 in Four Hours 2,500-Man VC Force Dealt Stunning Blow"

8 – William Comeau. Duel with the Dragon at the Battle of Suoi Tre, Deeds Publishing, First Edition, Copywrite 2022.

9 – Personal Story from Jim Hardin, 2nd/22nd Mechanized Infantry, 4th ID: "Suoi Tre – FSB Gold"

10 – Robert O. Babcock. War Stories – Utah Beach to Pleiku, Deeds Publishing,

Note: Bob Babcock served as an Infantry Platoon Leader in Vietnam in 1966-67 with Bravo Co, 1st/22nd Infantry, 4th ID.

## Chapter 10

1 – Personal Story from William Comeau, Alpha Co, 2nd/12th Infantry, 4th ID.

2 – Personal Story from William Comeau, Alpha Co, 2nd/12th Infantry, 4th ID: "Battle of Suoi Tre - Vietnam – 1967"

## Epilogue

1 - Merriam-Webster Dictionary

2 - Personal Story from William Comeau, Alpha Co, 2nd/12th Infantry, 4th ID.

## Appendix A

1 - Taken from the PUC Award

## Appendix B

1 - Personal Story from William Comeau, Alpha Co, $2^{nd}/12^{th}$ Infantry, $4^{th}$ ID: 3rd Brigade, 4ID and Suoi Tre,

July 17, 2023.

## Appendix C – More About Jon Palmer

Atkinson, Rick. The Long Gray Line: The American Journey of West Point's Class of 1966, Henry Holt and Company, LLC., Copyright 1989.

John F. Murray. Fallen Warriors – The West Point Class of 1964, Research Triangle Publishing, Inc., Copyright 1996.

Made in the USA
Monee, IL
10 January 2024

50513564R10098